A Man, a Boat, and Some Fish

Finding Your Identity so You Can Help Others Find Theirs

SETH SOKOLOFF

Copyright © 2017 by Seth Sokoloff

All rights reserved. This book or any portion thereof may not be reproduced or used in any manner whatsoever without the express written permission of the author except for the use of brief quotations in a book review.

ISBN: 1542537312
EAN-13: 9781542537315
Library of Congress Control Number: 2017907006
CreateSpace Independent Publishing Platform
North Charleston, South Carolina

Visit the author's website at http://www.sethsokoloff.org to order additional copies.

Scripture quotations marked (NLT) are taken from the Holy Bible, New Living Translation, copyright © 1996, 2004, 2007 by Tyndale House Foundation. Used by permission of Tyndale House Publishers, Inc., Carol Stream, Illinois 60188. All rights reserved.

Scripture quotations marked (NKJV) are taken from the New King James Version. Copyright © 1982 by Thomas Nelson, Inc. Used by permission. All rights reserved.

Scripture quotations marked (NIV) are taken from the Holy Bible, New International Version®, NIV® Copyright © 1973, 1978, 1984, 2011 by Biblica, Inc.® Used by permission. All rights reserved worldwide.

ACKNOWLEDGMENTS

I thought writing a book would be easy, but I quickly learned that this was not the case. This was by no means a Seth-only venture. Thank you to my wife, Diana, for always believing in me and being an editing master. My mom for being the first writer in the family and being such a great mom. Pastor Doug for continually planting the seed for writing and holding me accountable to actually do it. Pastors Bob and Sharon for all they have poured into me. Grace for designing an awesome cover while pregnant. Everyone who has been a part of my journey. Most importantly, thank you to the Lord for grabbing ahold of me and never letting go.

CONTENTS

Acknowledgments — iii
Foreword — vii
Preface — ix

1. A Man, a Boat, and Some Fish — 1
2. The Sea of Galilee (Repentance and Faith) — 8
3. Mending Nets (In My Own Power) — 17
4. Fisherman to Fisher of Men — 24
5. Unique as Only You Can Be — 34
6. Ensuring we are Disciples — 39
7. Changing When Others Want to Keep You in a Box — 47
8. Dealing with Failure — 56
9. Walking in a New Identity — 62
10. What about You? — 67

FOREWORD

There are two wonderful things I can tell you about Seth. One, he is one of the most intensely passionate and excellent young leaders I have ever met. Two, his love for the next generation is real and deep within him. A true love for the next generation will always translate into caring deeply about those who lead them. Caring for leaders means that you want them to discover their true God-given gifts. Once discovered, you pray that they lay those gifts back down at the feet of Jesus so that He can use and anoint them. Leaders who do this can be trusted to lead the next generation because it's not about possessing the gift but about fulfilling the call. We are all given gifts from God, but we choose to bring them back to Him.

When you love young people, you care about their leaders. I know this from twenty-two years of personal experience. The greatest joy in our lives has been seeing leaders like Seth and others ultimately bring their gifts back to Jesus so they can truly understand their existence on this earth. Each time Seth discovered something about himself or each time he accomplished something he did not think he could do, he brought that accomplishment back to Jesus for further instructions. This I admire.

Seth's journey has been miraculous. Period. We have sat for hours both Stateside and in Africa, laughing, crying, and listening to the stories of how the miraculous hand of God spared his life and guided his footsteps. I think the power of his testimony has equaled the radical nature of his call. I hope that one day he will write his testimony down with all of its miraculous twists and turns and its often hilarious mishaps.

A Man, a Boat, and Some Fish is Seth's statement to leaders, especially young leaders, to care for what God cares about. When he writes, "It is amazing what God can start with, especially in contrast to the end result," I know that he is so thankful for what God has done in his life. However, every day he is surrounded by many young people in Africa who feel as though they are underdogs living in the shadow of the West. Seth is giving them a real-life example of what God can do with anyone whose identity is in Christ. He is pleading with those who feel a call to lead to embrace the secret. What is the secret? If you know who you are in Christ, anything is possible. Focus on Jesus, your relationship with Him, and how He made you. Real power and authority, true Kingdom perspective, and an accurate understanding of the local church all begin with a proper identity. We all must discover our leadership at the feet of the one who designed us. Leading others is the greatest fruit of Jesus leading you.

This book is insightful, filled with proven principles for the young leader, and it gives a glimpse into the life of the writer. Read it with an open heart and mind. Make a list of things, as you read, that the Lord might be asking you to surrender. Be mindful of areas in your life where, as Seth describes, you need fresh water from the Holy Spirit flowing through you for strength and continued new life. There is no better place to start the journey than discovering who you are in Jesus.

When this young man expressed a desire to live in Africa for the rest of his life, to be used to impact a generation, and to be a part of building a strong healthy local church, I stared into his eyes, looking for something. I was looking for the idealism of youth, which can lead to disappointment. But what I saw along with idealism was a deep conviction of who he was and what God had called him to do. I have seen it in others over the years, and I know what it looks like. Now, looking back, I am proud to say that Seth and his wonderful wife, Diana, are fulfilling the exact call of God that he articulated to me over a cup of African coffee on the outskirts of Kampala, when he said, "I believe that God is calling me to reach the young people of this nation like never before." And so he is.

Pastor Doug Lasit
The Pearl Church
Denver, CO

PREFACE

When we look at our world today, it is so easy to jump to conclusions and declare situations as lost, hopeless, and beyond repair. Whether you think we are one step away from World War III or you believe the next world leader is the anti-Christ, it is easy to live life under the presumption that the worst is just around the corner. If this is the frame of reference, it is very hard to have any lasting vision that is worthwhile enough to change your life and how you view things.

Sure, you can see something or think up an idea that may garner your attention for a season. A vision that has the ability to change the very existence of your life and others can only be truly accepted if there is honest belief that not only situations but also you and those around you can change. I believe vision and identity go hand in hand. You cannot talk about one without talking about the other.

This book is about a lasting identity change given to us from the one who created our identity—the Lord. One that so radically changes our thinking that even how we see the world will be forever changed. I have considered the life of Simon Peter with creative liberty and looked at how an encounter with Jesus gave him a brand-new identity. Along with changing our identity, Jesus also wants to give us vision for our own lives and those around us. He wants us to be identity receivers and identity encouragers. My prayer is that your heart, as you read this book, would open to what the Lord would say to you. Often times we can easily teach these things to others around us, but as leaders it is equally, if not more important, to walk it out in our own lives.

I believe if you would allow God to speak to you, He will. God is the original vision setter. He is the one with the instruction manual for everything He made—from the smallest pebble to the biggest mind. Everything He created was created with purpose. The person He created to fulfill each purpose was specifically made for the vision He desires to set in front of them. There are no accidents, no mistakes, and certainly no visionless creations.

The joy in finding our identity is that, along with this great awakening, there is also an understanding of why we were created. Life without vision leads a person to not give any attention to who they are, why they are here, and what the point for today is. There is a lackadaisical view about all the pieces of life that leads to self-destruction in some and a contagious lull that sits on others. Whatever is set in front of you is the very thing that takes your attention. Anything that seems better (even if it is not) takes precedence over everything else. This may not be noticeable when things are going well, but the second a crisis comes, this fact becomes overwhelmingly apparent. Crisis either verifies the existence of vision or the large void of its absence. I have seen people with vision stand strong and unmoved in the greatest of trials, but I have also seen seemingly strong individuals shaken by the smallest of things. Vision rooted in a Christ-centered, Christ-initiated, and Christ-birthed identity has the ability to forever alter someone's existence, no matter how far lost he or she seems.

> And we know that all things work together for good to those who love God, to those who are the called according to His purpose. For whom He foreknew, He also predestined to be conformed to the image of His Son, that He might be the firstborn among many brethren. Moreover whom He predestined, these He also called; whom He called, these He also justified; and whom He justified, these He also glorified. (Rom. 8:28–30, NKJV)

So my question for you is, "Who are you, and why are you here?"

1

A MAN, A BOAT, AND SOME FISH

A man, a boat, and some fish. In all honesty, it was an uneducated man, a leaky old boat, and the occasional fish. In the eyes of most, this would sound like the beginning of a tragedy, not a story of hope. I've met some remarkable people in my life, and the things they have to offer to the world are a lot more glamorous looking than this: a degree, a full bank account, and a resume (CV) of success. It is amazing how quickly we judge a person by what we see or what they offer us. Often we also feel like we are being judged by others based on the same criteria. I wonder how many "poor fishermen" I have passed by just to strike up a conversation with someone who seems to have it a bit more together. It is curious how we process decisions, especially in relation to where we put our time, energy, and resources. What do we look at? Maybe more importantly, what do others see when they look at us? I am curious to know how many potential world leaders have been passed by simply because they didn't have the right credentials or didn't spend enough time shining their shoes before they left the house in the morning. People on the edge of certain groups and not at the center often make a tragic error. Instead of finding out who they are made to be, they change to try to match those closest to the center of what is considered the norm.

What exactly does it take to be a person who can change history? Do you need to be recognized or applauded by the right person? Is it possible to impact our world for an eternal and extraordinary goal, or is that a lofty aspiration reserved for a few? I believe life is not meant merely to exist. Life was created to fulfill something special—a purpose that only the unique life made by the Creator can complete. You are not an accident, a coincidence, or a random choice. There is a reason you and I are here. You are not a self-proclaimed leader; no mere person selected you. You are a leader called by God. To live a life that counts for eternity, you have to believe that it is divinely influenced from its inception. Sometimes it is the glaring contradiction of your beginning that catches you and others off guard. In reality, it doesn't matter what you or anyone else sees; it only matters what God sees! God's desire is for you to see what He sees.

It is amazing what God starts with, especially in contrast with the end result. I love reading biographies. Stories of great men and women who have lived in times past and how they came to do the things we remember them by excite me. One of the most striking things about most of these men and women is where they started their journeys. Most of them came out of situations that even the best author could not imagine. Some sound like a work of fiction, and I think that is what proves their truth. If you simply looked at what they had to offer with the human eye, the end result that we study in school today would look impossible.

Winston Churchill was sickly looking and considered dumb by his teachers and classmates. Yet he was exactly the man needed to lead an entire nation through war and help to defeat Hitler. Thomas Edison failed hundreds of times trying to invent one lightbulb. He was deaf and only had a few months of school to his name. Remarkably, through a series of failures, his invention still lights the planet today. Abraham Lincoln was born in a one-room house to parents who had never been to school. He began to read books at a young age in an attempt to educate himself. Not only did he become educated against all odds but he is today considered to be one of the greatest and most influential US presidents.

Look at the heroes of the Bible. Abraham was impatient and slept with his maid. David was an adulterer and murderer. Moses could not speak more than a few words without a stammer. Jonah literally ran from the Lord on a ship and thought he could hide from the all-seeing one. Paul persecuted Christians and the church. These lives are a history full of stories that I would have judged as failures. God spoke and declared that they were the perfect people for what He had called them to.

God looks at the same situations we see, but through drastically different lenses. He knows the very reasons He created each of us. God truly has the ability to choose and equip people from any circumstance and enable them to do literally anything He desires. He truly is the God of the impossible, and I think He has the most fun with those who have the least to offer. For me it was a bike, a hospital bed, and a lot of time to think. How about you? Maybe for you, it is right now: a book, a table, and a chair. What is it that you have (perhaps insignificant to you) that God wants to use?

A man, a boat, and some fish.

This is what a man named Simon had to offer. Countless times he had been labeled the exact same way: "Oh, you mean that dumb guy who can't catch fish and who always spends time in that old boat?" Simon may not have even noticed how bad his situation looked from the other side. He may not even have been able to come up with a single point on a list if you asked him what he had to offer. In fact he may have pointed you to his brothers or perhaps his father. Maybe they would know. His identity was not one he chose but one that was given to him by others. The problem was that his identity didn't quite fit right.

I have met many young leaders who have spent more time trying to be like one of the rock-star preachers they have seen at a large conference than they have spent trying to find who God has made them to be. Our culture worldwide, and more and more the culture in the church, is tirelessly trying hard to hurl its ideal identity on us as leaders. If we are not careful, we can allow this to take prominence over the identity God wants to give us. To some extent it is good to desire to be like proven men and women of God, but only to the level of making us become better leaders seeking after the Lord—not better imitators of the next big thing.

Simon was very many things, but a fisher of fish he was not. It is likely that Simon's father, and his father, and *his* father's father were all fishermen. I do not know if the inability to catch fish was passed down but certainly the career choice was. His brothers set out to fish each morning just as he did. This was by far what was normal for most families of that day. Simon woke up early each morning; ventured to the seaside; prepared his boat, his nets, and some small bread for lunch; and launched out into the water. This was what he was supposed to do. This was his life and the only life he knew.

Every day of his recent memory was probably eerily similar to the previous one. It was often hot and, except for the occasional storm, calm and monotonous. The story might have been different if Simon had been interrupted regularly with a huge catch of fish. Perhaps he dreamed of a career change, but right now it seemed that nothing would change—ever. Each passing day, his point of reference became more and more blurred by the overwhelming monotony of his current situation. It was becoming harder to form any concept of moving forward. Simon's daily routine was closing in on him from all sides, and he needed a new point of reference. He needed a starting point. Something he could once again look back on and see how far he had come. Something to help him measure future progress.

When we struggle with our identity as a leader, it is easy to lose heart for where God has placed us. Identity crisis can lead to seeking an exit. If I am not moving forward, maybe I should just move on. My prayer is that throughout the next few chapters, God will not only give you a new starting point but also give an entirely fresh passion for your God-ordained identity. That identity will empower you to help others find and walk in their identity also.

I often times find it hard to see progress in things I am working on in my life. The longer the journey, the more difficult it is to see any change. In relation to the end result, a year, a season, or a step can seem incidental to the end goal. Whenever I fly between Uganda and the United States, I am always reminded of how hard it is to recognize progress. When I look at the map on the screen in front of me, a few hours in a long sixteen-hour flight seem like we have not made any progress at all. The tiny little cartoon plane seems to stay in the same spot. The screaming baby, limited leg room, and overzealous flight attendants are all constant reminders of how far I still have to travel. In a journey as big as life, sometimes the best way to measure ground gained is to make where we started our point of reference from which to measure change, not the seemingly impossible destination.

Sometimes we get discouraged looking at our present surroundings, our eyes fixed on our current place in time, which is seemingly not different from last week or last month. In fact, most of the time, we can even think we are taking steps backward instead of forward. We look at others and how far they have moved in what seems like such a short amount of time compared to us. It seems so overwhelming, but just like David the giant killer, we need to be led to a place that allows us to see from a perspective that is different—a different vantage point. I sometimes need to leave my seat and walk around the plane a bit. By getting up I can see people handling the same situation differently. I can see the ground moving outside of the window. I can talk to other travelers who just got off a twenty-hour flight or thirty-hour layover. Others help me see the things I currently cannot. All of a sudden my view changes. I see my journey completely differently than I had before.

> When my heart is overwhelmed; lead me to the rock that
> is higher than I. (Ps. 61:2, NKJV)

Try to put yourself in David's shoes while he is writing these words. Historians think Psalm 61 was written during his exile from his son Absalom while he was in the desert. David's own son had taken the kingdom from under him. He had humiliated him in front of an entire nation, and now David was stuck trying to process the week's events. David was hiding for his life in a cave. Progress? Forward moving? If anything, David must have thought he moved twenty steps backward to a place even further back than when Samuel anointed him king. He had no kingdom, family, or sense of future. Any plans he had were now completely shrouded by this glaring possibility that he may never set foot in his own kingdom again. From deep down somewhere, he was able to muster this simple prayer. Although he could not see anything with his natural eyes from where he was standing, God was more than able to show him so much more from a different place, a rock that was higher than him...Jesus.

I used to live in a little town that was surrounded by the Cascade Mountain range. Each peak had a different name. On a clear day, you could see mountains as far as the eye could see in any direction. If you were a true local, you could name all of them. Once in a while, I would drive to the base of one and climb up it as far up as I could. Sometimes I climbed with friends, but most often alone with a lot of things on my mind. There is something about being high up, in the middle of nowhere, where the only living things around are trees, that allows you to see things differently. To be outside of normal and able to look into the exact same situation just from a different angle suddenly changes things. My circumstances did not change, but how I looked at them did. At times we have to be called out to leave where we are. Life can become so consuming that an outside force is needed in order for us to stop what we are doing and look around. It is only when I leave where I am and position myself to look back to where I started that I can truly see and testify that God can do so much with so little. I really have come a long way.

Ministry can be overwhelming. It is hard to measure the pressure a pastor or leader faces. In the heat of a season, we can think we are doing great when deep down we are barely holding on. People have problems and issues that get thrown upon us from all sides. Other leaders have expectations and demands. We ourselves are continually trying to challenge ourselves to be a better follower of Christ and a better helper of those around us. If we don't take time to sit and realize that (1) we are under a lot of pressure and (2) we need to keep a careful watch over our own souls, we can find ourselves beaten down. We need to take time to anchor ourselves in the Lord and what He is doing in our lives. We are winning, and we are making progress. Where we are today is not where we started.

Simon probably didn't even know he was searching for a fresh start, but it found him where he was—in a boat with a net in hand, going about his day. It was here when the person he had only heard rumors about came. Jesus gave him a simple command attached to a promise that must have been so shocking and reassuring at the same time, "Follow Me and I will make you a fisher of men." Sometimes the simplest of things have the potential to speak volumes to us. Little did Simon know in that moment, but everything up to this point in his life had been pointing him to this very juncture. I can imagine him looking down at his hands and what was around him and asking, "Me?" Certainly there must have been a mistake! This is Jesus whose reputation preceded Him, talking to Simon whose reputation was simply nonexistent. In his heart, Simon must have thought this was all a big mistake and once Jesus realized it, he would move on. To the contrary, somehow the closer Christ came, the more certain and intently He looked. "No really, Follow Me."

"But all I have to offer is me…a man, a boat, and some fish."

2

THE SEA OF GALILEE
(REPENTANCE AND FAITH)

Who or what defined Simon's identity? The people around him, changing circumstances, and his failures all crowded in and attempted to define him. Most of his daily routines were connected to one thing in particular: the Sea of Galilee. But this very water that defined Simon's identity also frustrated him. In a life-changing moment, it was on the shores of this sea where Simon met Jesus.

The Sea of Galilee is a large body of water that is actually a lake. It is located at the northern tip of Israel and is fed by the Jordan River from the north. It is the largest freshwater lake in Israel and has the lowest sitting elevation of any lake in the world. This body of water is a lifeline for the entire region and truly gives identity to the people living on its shores. I can imagine locals wearing T-shirts when they travel other places that read, "I am Galilee." Local peddlers carry refrigerator magnets, postcards, and other tourist souvenirs as they walk along the shores!

For centuries, Israelites gathered their water for drinking, cooking, and bathing from this lake. Any village even remotely close to it was sustained by the commerce the lake provided. Fishermen work, earn a living, and eat from its waters. Taxi operators ferry people and goods between its shores. Families play and vacation on its beaches. An entire people group seemed unwittingly dependent on a commodity that they felt was guaranteed. The lake had always been there, why would that ever change? Honestly, who worries about a natural landmark disappearing? There are certain things in life that I do not have on my prayer list. "Lord, keep the ocean water flowing" is something I can honestly say I have never prayed. Often in life we take for granted the things that are in front of us. The presence of this lake was constant and assumed just like the air they breathed. We often do not appreciate that God uses our environment or unquestioned circumstances to show us who He is and to help teach us who He wants us to be.

> For since the creation of the world His invisible attributes are clearly seen, being understood by the things that are made, even His eternal power and Godhead, so that they are without excuse. (Rom. 1:20, NKJV)

We are not where we are by accident. We are certainly not where we are for no purpose. God simply does not work that way. In each season as leaders, no matter where we find ourselves, God wants to teach us something new about who He is and who He is making us to be. Lurking under the surface of this permanent sea is an unseen bubbling reminder that there is someone in control of everything.

A series of underground saltwater springs flow into the sea along with the Jordan River. The weight of the fresh water holds the salt water flowing underneath at bay. On the surface it may seem like any other freshwater lake, but its true identity is found at the bottom, deep inside. The freshwater lake is actually a salty relative to the infamous Dead Sea. The Dead Sea is given its name because the high salt content makes it unable to sustain any life. The life-giving Sea of Galilee is actually only a drought away from becoming the dead Sea of Galilee. Today the Sea of Galilee is at a historically dangerous low. Less and less fresh water is flowing into it, and the salt water is trying to tip the balance scale. This is a situation that if not reversed could result in the salt water taking over the fresh water, and the lake would then no longer be able to sustain life and commerce.

This change would be hard to reverse and would become a new normal. At any time, the Lord could decide that a change was necessary. The fresh water could give way to the salt water, and life for an entire region would change in an instant. This slow, but continual, change in identity of the Sea of Galilee would also end up affecting the identity of everyone who lived near the lake.

Just like this example of the Sea of Galilee, there are many who look to you as a role model and source of identity. Indiscretions and struggles that we have are often passed on to those who we lead. It is no coincidence that when a leader falls, the ones they are leading struggle with their faith as well. It is so important that we understand and are vigilant to ensure that we know who we are and deal with the things that would try to disrupt God's vision for our life. Repentance helps keep the wrong sources of things that would alter our identity out of our lives, while faith ensures that we are trusting God to do the changing.

Repentance
The Sea of Galilee is in a constant state of identity crisis, and I think leaders face this kind of test far too often. There is too much salt water flowing into our lives and if not reversed could lead to this life-giving source of leadership no longer able to sustain life. As leaders many of us have plenty of fresh water flowing in. We read the Bible, pray, worship, and encourage others to do the same. For some it may be a mere trickle of poisonous salty water, while for others it may have become a gushing flow but still hidden and not observable by those around. Often times the biggest enemy to our identity is the outside thing that we allow to influence us. This could be sin, idolatry, attitudes, or the wrong source of influence. These streams, if not stopped, could begin to change what we were meant to be. Whether we know it or not we influence many around us. These streams could lead us from being life givers to those who surround us, or to being the complete opposite. Simon, like the Sea of Galilee, was unaware of just how much of the wrong flow he was allowing in.

Hidden sin is one of the ugliest growth stunters and identity stealers. As leaders it may be difficult to admit that we struggle with sin. Maybe we don't feel that we have a safe place to confess. But when things remain hidden in the dark, they have power over us. It is only when they are revealed and brought into the light that they can be dealt with. The Sea of Galilee's hidden secret, if left unexposed, could never have the chance to be rectified. Now that it has been discovered, steps are being taken to protect it. We need to constantly pray David's prayer and ask that the Lord show us any flow of salt water (sin) in our lives and help us to be honest to deal with it. Then we can maintain our fresh water and effectiveness in leading others and fulfilling the call that God has placed on each one of us.

> Search me, O God, and know my heart; try me, and know my anxieties. And see if there is any wicked way in me, and lead me in the way everlasting. (Ps. 139:23–24, NKJV)

Idolatry was the flow of contaminating salt water that the Israelites never dealt with. They set other things above God in their lifestyle, in their affection, and most importantly in their hearts. They sought to emulate the ways of others, from their speech to the things they worshipped. They even married other nation's women and adopted their traditions. As young leaders, it is so easy to look at celebrity-Christians and idolize them. We strive to be more like them in an attempt to gain the fruit that we think they have. I have heard young preachers change their preaching style to sound more like someone else. Someone wears an outfit at a conference, and sooner or later everyone is doing the same. This is idolatry and results in exchanging a God-given identity for something that doesn't fit. Simon was called to be a fisherman, but not a fisher of fish, rather a fisher of men.

> Who may ascend into the hill of the Lord? Or who may stand in His holy place? He who has clean hands and a pure heart, who has not lifted up his soul to an idol, nor sworn deceitfully. (Ps. 24:3–4, NKJV)

Allowing negativity to impact us is another source of salt water for many of us. As a leader, especially of young people, there is such pressure to be relevant. We must seek a balance in this area. I do not think we should be so cut off from our culture that we become weird. Being disconnected can lead to having no common ground with those we are ministering to. This being said, I think it is possible to be informed, but not influenced, by popular culture. We can know who a musical artist is and still not know even one of their songs. We can understand the premise of a movie without ever seeing it. The biggest influence and source of our ability to relate must be the Bible. The people we lead should be able to look at our lives and see a model of what it looks like to be set apart and not one that looks like everyone else. They don't need to see what it looks like to be a world-focused person who is also a Christian. They need to see a Christian who is totally focused on redeeming their world. Our standards and personal convictions should exceed those around us because we live in a culture with such low personal standards and convictions of right and wrong. Our standards and convictions must be God initiated and maintained by repentance.

> I do not pray that You should take them out of the world, but that You should keep them from the evil one. They are not of the world, just as I am not of the world. Sanctify them by Your truth. Your word is truth. As You sent Me into the world, I also have sent them into the world. And for their sakes I sanctify Myself, that they also may be sanctified by the truth. (John 15:17–19, NKJV)

Living a lifestyle of repentance is the only way to keep the contamination of salt water from flowing into our lives. This lifestyle of openness is being constantly aware of where we are as individuals and being willing to acknowledge our weak areas. We need to be able to come before the Lord for His forgiveness and help. As a leader I have often been told that a leader is one who is also being led. Leaders need to have people in their lives whom they can be accountable to in every area. This also applies to repentance. A good question to ask is, "When was the last time I repented of anything?" If you can't remember the last time, this may be an area to take to the Lord.

> Repent therefore and be converted, that your sins may be blotted out, so that times of refreshing may come from the presence of the Lord. (Acts 3:19, NKJV)

Repentance is a foundational stone. The only way we can find our true identity is to allow God to be the loudest voice in our lives. The moment we stop allowing our areas of weakness to be exposed and corrected is the very moment we as leaders stop being just that…leaders! Leaders are only true leaders when they are also being led. God's vision for you and me is so much greater than what we can see with our natural eyes. The world is desperately in need of leaders who have been so removed from wrong influences that all that remains is what God has spoken to them.

What is God calling you to be?

Faith
The Sea of Galilee also speaks to the area of faith. All of us have a measure of unquestioning trust in certain things just like the inhabitants around the Sea of Galilee. We have a blind faith that when we step out of bed in the morning, the floor will hold our weight; when we open the curtains, the sun will be shining. We rarely give a second thought to these things because natural laws guarantee them. We don't stop and recognize it, but believer or atheist, we have faith in something bigger than ourselves. We can't make the earth spin any faster than it is currently spinning. Nor can we make the tides of the sea rise or fall. No matter how smart, established, or influential we are, there is someone much bigger than you and me in control. It is this kind of innate faith in the unfailing laws of nature that God wants us to have in Him. Faith not only in the sea but also in the creator of its banks, waters, and fish. The creator of you and me!

It is at this very sea that Jesus stood and spoke to those seated on its banks. The message he intentionally chose was the parable of the sower (Matt. 13). Jesus spoke to a people who understood fishing and farming. They believed that they were the ones in control. Jesus reminded them that the same seeds could be planted in different locations, and while some would flourish, others would shrivel and die. Paul used this analogy later in the New Testament, acknowledging that man can plant, tend, and water with all his expertise, but it is God who ultimately gives the seed life and makes it grow.

> Who then is Paul, and who is Apollos, but ministers through whom you believed, as the Lord gave to each one? I planted, Apollos watered, but God gave the increase. (1 Cor. 3:5–6, NKJV)

It is meaningful that Jesus used this relevant example of God's sovereignty in sowing and reaping as he stood on the shores of the Sea of Galilee—a sea where God has sovereignly kept the water fresh. Jesus did not just use words that made sense to their minds but stood next to a living example that they could see with their eyes. This is the same God who brings forth life from our mundane, dead situations like the one in which Simon, the washed up fisherman, found himself.

This is the very God and the very sea where earlier Simon's name was called out. Jesus came and gave definition to the faith that Simon had in his identity as a fisherman on the Sea of Galilee. Jesus called Simon to a higher faith in someone bigger than what he could create on his own—a life-giving, life-changing God. Simon's identity was now to be grounded on a permanent call, one that waves, family influence, fear, or even boredom could not move. Simon's faith was not to be in something that was fooling everyone like the Sea of Galilee but on the solid, unwavering rock, Jesus Christ.

Simon was unaware that God had been part of his life from the beginning. His name, the year and location of his birth, the family in which he was raised, and the choice to be a fisherman were no accident. Even the water in which he fished was literally sustained by God!

God is in control!

I grew up in a home without a father in sight. From my earliest memories, I remember asking the question, "Why?" Very often the answer that follows this question isn't one that we want to hear. The worst answer to me is a nonanswer: "Because I said so!" For a long time, my question went unanswered. All my friends seemed to have a father; every kid on TV seemed to have a father. Why not me? Surely God didn't intentionally make me suffer with this huge hole in my heart?

After I got saved, the Lord began to work healing in this area of my life. God became my father, and He also brought natural fathers into my life through the church community. Still the question of "Why me?" was never answered. It wasn't until years down the road that I moved to Uganda and found myself working in the middle of a generation that has been called the Fatherless Generation. Uganda has the highest number of young people per capita in the world, and a vast majority of them have not had a father at home. Suddenly, one of my biggest questions was answered. God had been working in my life all along. He truly was working all things for good.

> And we know that all things work together for good to those who love God, to those who are the called according to His purpose. (Rom. 8:28, NKJV)

It is so easy to be ignorant of God working in our lives. It is one of the enemies' greatest lies to make us believe that God is at work in everyone else's life but not in mine. We begin to think that we are alone in the midst of a huge confusing world. I am sure that Simon felt this way as he sat alone in a boat surrounded by nothing but a vast sea of familiar water. He was oblivious to the secret at the bottom of the Sea of Galilee. Why was he a fisherman here? Simon knew of a God in heaven, but not a God on earth, not a God who is alive and at work in his day-to-day life.

As with any good Jewish boy, he had knowledge of how God had worked with his ancestors. He had heard the great stories. But what about him? Why was he alive? Would anything ever change? Could God use someone like Simon? More importantly, the question is, Can God use someone like me...someone like you?

One of the first steps to lasting change is faith. Faith to believe that change is possible! Many of us don't believe that we can really change. There is a deep-rooted fear that I am stuck the way that I am forever. It takes faith to believe that Jesus is the Christ. It takes faith to obey and leave all that I am doing when He says, "Follow me." Simon had to leave a life of self-sustenance and exchange it for an unknown life of becoming a "fisher of men."

Years later, after Jesus's death and promised resurrection, he met Simon again on the shores of the Sea of Galilee (John 21) and gave Simon a fresh start, total forgiveness, and reaffirmation of his call and destiny. I find it interesting that there are so many biblical greats who experienced the beginning or fulfillment of their ministry in the context or setting of water: the calling and commissioning of Simon Peter, Jesus's first miracle, Moses passing the baton to Joshua, Elisha receiving the mantle from Elijah, and John the Baptist heralding Jesus. Water is a picture of newness. It washes, cleanses, and sustains life.

Repentance leads us to change, and faith helps us believe that Christ is able to make the change last. Just like Simon, we all have our own Sea of Galilee, where God wants to deal with our identity. God is the author of who we were made to be. There are many things that try to come against our God-given identity. Sometimes it is external forces and things that stand in our way, but often we are the ones who get in the way the most!

3

MENDING NETS (IN MY OWN POWER)

Most likely Simon's boat was an old hand-built, wooden fishing vessel made out of cedar from Lebanon. It probably was older and had been owned and used by his father. Simon was part of the family business, earning income for his family unit as a whole. The boat most likely came with a couple of slow leaks that required continual attention. He no doubt had to go between fishing and scooping water from the boat back into the sea. There was no time for rest or simple enjoyment; he was in a constant state of busyness, keeping the boat afloat.

I have spent some time on similar, older, hand-made fishing boats here in Uganda. It is amazing how much confidence the owners have in them even though there is nothing confidence inspiring about them. Even the newly made ones look like antiques. Mostly, I have been the passenger as the journey unfolded in a predictable way. Within a few minutes of departure, the owner who was driving the boat would throw me some sort of bailing (water-removing) device such as an old water bottle or bucket. With broken English and hand gestures, he would then mime removing water from the bottom of the boat and throwing it into the lake. For the next several hours, this became my lot in life. I pride myself at being a master bailer—scooping water out of the boat only to watch it come rushing back in! The leaks appear anywhere, from the top to the bottom, from the front to the back as an endless stream into the less and less trusty old boat. This "kitchen strainer" is considered to be a boat in good condition because it only requires a single person to bail full time, not two. This is normal, and compared to the vast number of fishermen on the lake, the accident rate is lower than one would expect. This statistic is almost unbelievable after riding in one of these boats.

Staying afloat is a full-time job, one that these fishermen think is normal. Only those of us experiencing this for the first time might question its practicality. How often is this true for many areas of our lives? We are so used to some of our struggles that it is only someone looking from outside who can see the problem. Instead of surviving by continual bailing of water to stay afloat, we need someone to help us bail or better yet, fix our boat.

As leaders, I don't think we realize how much we must shoulder on a regular basis.

First and most importantly, we must keep ourselves in a life-giving relationship with the Lord. We must be free from sin, growing daily, staying teachable, and so on. We must fight to ensure that our relationship with the Lord is growing. When things get hard, the temptation is to allow this area to take the back seat to give room for other "good and godly" things. It takes effort and adds to the weight we carry to keep this foundational area of personal growth a priority. Without this, it is not a question of if we will fail, but when. I have witnessed and heard stories of incredibly gifted leaders buckling under the weight of ministry. Sadly, one of the common denominators in most of these stories is a slow leak in the area of personal time spent with Jesus. We need to be aware of the fact that this area is a part of the leadership weight that we carry.

In addition to fulfilling the most important responsibility we just discussed, we must also serve those we lead. We feel the burden of their walk with the Lord; we carry their struggles, pains, and hurts. We fail to let others help us carry the weight, and we find ourselves struggling to stay afloat. What we don't realize is that this survival attempt is changing who we are. Instead of the victorious leaders God made us to be, we become those barely surviving.

During this past season, Life Church in Uganda has been going through a senior-pastor transition. I am convinced that everything that can be shaken during a transition will be, and a very wise person told me, "No one goes through unscathed." At times during this transition, I found myself simply trying to stay afloat. Not enough rest, too much pride, or a number of other factors I'm sure, led me to function more and more in my own power. That proved to not be enough! In actuality, my identity began to change. I became a survivor, seeking pity and forgetting who God made me to be. Our own power will never be enough.

Let's understand that life and its demands are constantly trying to affect who we are. I have met lots of people who have allowed circumstances to define them. Part of Simon's journey was sifting through what life had made him, and allowing God to speak newness into those needy or hurting areas. Simon wasn't perfect at this, and he had a propensity to allow life to rekindle old identity beliefs in him. He needed to see that he couldn't fight this in his own power. Jesus helped Simon realize that he wasn't created to simply float in his boat, but that in a miracle moment his boat could be full of fish. Jesus wanted to help Simon walk hand-in-hand with his creator and go from merely surviving to thriving in life. This is only possible when we allow God to help us surrender *our* pursuits for *His*.

Complete Newness

Imagine with me as Simon, in addition to using his old, experienced boat, also managed with an older net, one with innumerable holes repaired through the years. Sometimes the repair was well done, and sometimes it was done in haste as he was pressured to catch something to show for his day's work. Anything handy such as pieces of older nets, stray lengths of string, even personal clothing might have made its way into the repair job. The net became a mosaic of random articles that represented a story. Children would gather in anticipation to watch the fishermen on the shore after a day's work. As children do, they would ask, "What happened here?"

so they could hear the story of each needed repair. As a good Jewish, I am sure none of Simon's tales would have been embellished at all! Although Simon seemed heroic to the children, deep down Simon wondered if the net would hold a full catch of fish. There was faith needed for the daily tugging of the net out of the water. But the reality was, Simon rarely tested the integrity of the net as time after time he pulled out nothing more than a few objects left by other fishermen.

What a picture of the way we were before we encountered Christ standing on the shore of our lives. Our own human efforts were continually at work to make, keep afloat, and fix our lives. Our lives were covered with our own fingerprints in ignorant attempts to keep pushing blindly ahead, all the while testifying to the fruit of our own ambition.

Having repaired many things by myself, I can look back at each repair and see the lack of uniformity it holds. Repairs never look exactly the same as the original. People make entire careers out of trying to mask brokenness and make it look like new. But real experts can always tell when there has been a repair. No matter how good the work, it can't stand up to the ultimate test: being held next to an original. There is always a mark of the repairer and the material used to repair. You may be the best fixer to have ever fixed, but you will never be able to match the one who created the original.

We need to rethink what it means to be made new. We often consider newness in our lives as God repairing the broken things: putting some filler and some new paint on the cracks that reveal our brokenness. We want our past hurts to be fixed, plastered over, so no one can see that there was ever a problem. However, merely covering up an issue never fully heals it and hiding a past area of brokenness eliminates its potential to be used as an example to encourage or influence anyone else. There is a better way.

Where our lives are bearing the marks of brokenness or attempted fix jobs, we need the Creator to come and fashion something totally new. He will remake our lives so that the broken parts from before are not recognizable. Our lives are so beautiful and unique and God will fashion us to be exactly what He wants, so we will be useful. The marks become a tapestry of all our experiences working together as a magnificent testimony of what the Creator can do with a broken, torn net.

"Repaired" things are never as valuable as the original. Imagine you are buying a used car and the previous owner explains that it had been in an accident but you shouldn't worry because it was repaired well. No matter how good the repair, you would demand a reduction in price because a repaired item is never as valuable as an original. One of my favorite things is to see people who take old, broken things and make brand-new things out of them. I have seen furniture made out of old engine parts, entire homes built from old pieces of barns, and everything in between. These items, contrary to repaired items, demand a much higher price than the standard ones. They are considered art and one-of-a-kind pieces—unique. They haven't simply been fixed; they have been completely refashioned into something new!

As leaders, we need to continually embrace the things that have made us who we are. We know the journey that has brought us to where we are today and the things that have led us to act the way we do. God wants to use those things in order to shape us into the person He wants us to be. In our own ambition, we can try to force different experiences into usable sermon illustrations or try to give meaning to things, but God doesn't want to simply reconcile those experiences for us. He wants to use those experiences to make us into something totally new.

Jesus stood on the shore of the Sea of Galilee and called to Simon. He called Simon to put down his broken net and old boat and allow Him to make something new of Simon's life. Jesus called Simon to no longer be a self-maintaining, failing fisher of fish but become a God-thriving, successful fisher of men. This is a legacy and story recorded for all of us to read.

What can God do with a man, a boat, and some fish? He can make something new, not something to simply maintain but something He can use. We need to allow Jesus to take complete control of every aspect of our lives. When we surrender to what He wants in our lives, we will experience lasting newness and change from the inside out.

Who's the Boss?

I enjoy being in control. To some extent, we all enjoy being in control. Even though it may be difficult at times, we enjoy having the final say as to what happens in our lives. What we fail to realize is that in our own power our life will only be as good as we can make it. No matter how talented we are as leaders, we were not destined to lead our own lives. We were made to follow Jesus and lead others to do the same. In order for our lives to be all that God has planned, we have to give up control completely to Him.

Simon found himself at a crossroads with the Lord. Up to this point, his life had been dictated by his own desires. Jesus was now asking him to leave all that he had made in his own power and experience all that Christ had for him. I'm sure there was a moment of weighing the options and honestly thinking about what exactly this would mean. He would be giving up everything he had spent his entire life up to this point trying to create. There must have been something in the confidence of Christ's offer. A glimmer of hope and trust exploded within Simon, our dear fisherman, as he handed over the reins of his life to Christ. Simon agreed to no longer be a fisher of fish but to become what he was created to be: a fisher of men.

The original Greek word for "left" that is used in Simon's story in Matthew 4:20 is the same word as "forgiveness." Being forgiven literally means to "lay down" and leave the thing we were carrying. Accepting the Lord's forgiveness and choosing to follow Him means we must lay down the burden of leading our own lives. We need to lay down our control in order to pick up all that the Lord has for us. The Lord has set these things in front of us, and He is waiting for us to pick them up. We cannot pick up anything if our hands are full of our own lives. We need to lay them down in order to free our hands to hold all that Christ offers.

As a leader, I believe the call is going out to you and me. Have we achieved where we are at by ourselves or has God been in divine control? The areas we feel like we are most in control are the very areas God wants us to surrender so that it is no longer what success I have achieved but what I have allowed God to control. Our identity as leaders is not something that we should create, but rather it must be started, maintained, and brought to fulfillment by God himself. Simon did not go from fishing fish to fishing men by simply deciding to. God spoke to him and then led and enabled him to make this change.

4

FISHERMAN TO FISHER OF MEN

Have you ever looked back at old pictures of yourself and had the thought, "What on earth was I thinking…? Whoever told me those pants were cool? I begged my mom for weeks to get that haircut…I wish she hadn't let me."

In Uganda, when you visit someone's house, you are usually met with the host's stack of photos from their life so that you can look at them while tea, or whatever they will serve you, is being prepared. A few weeks prior to writing this, I was at someone's home and sure enough, the photos were deposited in my lap. While looking at the pictures, and enjoying the stories the host told me, a strange thing happened. After every few pictures, he swooped in and grabbed one out of my hand, explaining that I wasn't supposed to see that one, that it was before he was saved, and so forth. He was obviously embarrassed by what he used to be and had not yet "edited" the story of his past. He thought that in order to have a new identity today, he had to pretend that past things never happened.

I definitely have things in my past that I am not proud of. I, too, was not saved for a good part of my younger life. I made decisions that resulted in consequences I still deal with today. When I received Jesus as my Lord and Savior, I felt 100 percent cleansed of everything I had ever done. I became a new creation. I was born again and became a Christian. Still, the photos in my photo album remain there. There is still physical proof of what I was before I was a follower of Jesus. For a long time, I wanted to filter all of it out like my friend with his photo album. I wanted to act like none of it ever happened, and just as Christ forgets my past, I wanted to follow suit. I wanted a new identity.

Simon is one of my favorites in the Bible. He was just like us. He was a normal guy who made errors just like we do. Simon had his identity dictated to him by others. Even if he desired to be something else, his family background destined him to be a fisherman. He bore the photos of many past generations in his life's album. This caused him to make some decisions that later in life didn't look as they had in the moment. His identity was formed by everything around him and was confirmed by his mistakes along the way. It seemed like he was fighting a losing battle. His photo album was being filled with memories that at some point reached a tipping point. Finally, the issue was no longer how to stop the inflow of these memories but how to deny and destroy their existence. The temptation is strong to hide past memories and pretend that they never happened. The problem is, when we hide them, they not only continue to hold influence in our lives, but as much as we don't want to be associated with them, they secretly change our identity from the inside out. Hidden things always hold power over us. It is only when we bring things into the open that we can handle them in a godly way, and God can actually use them for good.

In our culture today, it is extremely hard, some would even say impossible, to not be influenced by media and the Internet. Everywhere you look, there is someone living the perfect life, and declaring that by some magic solution, you can do the same. You just need a new pair of jeans, or know what words to use in a conversation. Culture tells you that you are not good enough, but if you simply pretend to be someone else, maybe then you will fit in. People's identities are no longer their own. The problem is the person they are trying to be like is most likely trying to be like someone else as well. We are facing an identity crisis! I believe that God has made you unique, with special deposits of characteristics that only you have. The reason you have these is because only the you whom God made can accomplish the call that is on your life. Sadly for most, this identity

God so uniquely created, is hidden behind what everyone else wants to see. People are fighting to keep up an image that they were never meant to have. It is exhausting and is keeping so many from truly living the life they were created for.

Simon was created to be more than a fisherman. No one ever told him this, so he simply shut down any thoughts of a bigger vision for his life. When he was old enough, he apprenticed under his dad and learned the tools of the trade. He learned the best time of day to fish, how weather and seasons affected fish, the type of nets to use, and how to row a boat without the fish sensing the movement! He had a doctorate in fishing by the time he was done. He knew all there was to know…the only problem was he was never meant to be a fisher of fish.

This was continually made clear to him. All his friends were great at catching fish, but Simon never quite got it. He always seemed to leave the shore a few minutes too late. He used a white net on the day a brown net was working. He rowed left, when everyone knew it was better to go right. The years passed, and he became more and more frustrated with his inability to fish. He concluded that he was a failure, and he should give up though he never knew why he felt that way. Then one day, everything changed.

Simon had just returned from another day of working hard and catching nothing. He was exhausted, his clothes smelled, and he was near his wit's end. Out of nowhere, a man appeared and told him to try one more time. I don't know about you, but you could not have paid me enough to get back in that boat and try again. A hot shower, a bowl of ice cream, and some ridiculous movie would be the only thing I would be thinking about. On top of that, this guy obviously hadn't the slightest clue about fishing. He was not wearing the clothes of a fisherman, and he certainly didn't know the language fishermen use. Why should Simon listen to this man? But for whatever reason, Simon got back in the boat and tried one more time. He did just as the man said. Miraculously, he caught so many fish with so little effort that the catch began to sink the boat (Matt. 4, Luke 5).

At that moment, Simon realized two things:

1. If fishing were truly this easy, he had no idea what he was doing.
2. This man was no ordinary man; He was Jesus, the Christ.

When they finally got the sinking boat to shore, Simon fell on his knees before Jesus and told him to leave him alone because he was a sinful man. He had years of photos to prove it. Simon knew that anyone who knew him could confirm what a bad person he was. Jesus simply looked at Simon and said, "Follow me."

A moment in the presence of Jesus enabled Simon to throw off a lifetime of a man-made, man-sustained image. Simon left his boat, his nets, his newly found fortune, and most importantly, his identity as a fisherman to follow the man who had come to find him. What caused a man with a lifetime of investment into his faulty identity to forsake it in a matter of seconds?

> Now the Lord is the Spirit; and where the Spirit of the Lord is, there is liberty. But we all, with unveiled face, beholding as in a mirror the glory of the Lord, are being transformed into the same image from glory to glory, just as by the Spirit of the Lord. (2 Cor. 3:17–18, NKJV)

Where God is, there is a freedom to be who He made you to be. There is no image to uphold because God knows everything. He knows you are not who you are pretending to be. He sees you as the completed one He made. His very countenance projects that image onto you. We look into His face and see ourselves filtered through Him looking back at us. We are being transformed from glory to glory into His image…His identity created for us!

In a moment Jesus showed Simon a picture of what He was making him to be. Simon had the action, the tenacity, and even half of the name correct, but his goal was wrong. He wasn't called to catch fish but to catch people. Jesus didn't discredit everything he had spent his life doing. Instead, Jesus took his life and gave it a new focus. As leaders, our identity is rooted in the things that God has brought us through. Our experiences, passions, hope, and dreams all align when God reveals the purpose for which He created us. A fisherman was becoming a fisher of men!

Failure to understand and embrace our identity in Christ leads to an area that I have seen most negatively affect Christian leaders today… insecurity.

Insecurity

Insecurity is truly a silent killer. It shows itself in so many insidious ways: a feeling that the people around you are not receiving you like they once did, an anxiety that you have to try to earn their acceptance again even though in truth you never lost it, a concern that you are not good enough, and that at any moment things are going to come crashing down around you. Insecurity can lead people to act awkwardly and be guarded. Eventually it can ruin a person's influence and relationships. Insecurity robs us of our true identity.

This is not the will of God for those who are following Him. Like we talked about earlier, Christ wants us, above all else, to be sure of our identity in Him. I have often heard that insecurity is one of the worst forms of pride in a leader. If not guarded and cultivated, our view of who we are and the source of our confidence shifts away from God to what we receive from other people. The source of our life and identity changes. We begin to seek after other sources of acceptance and change from being confident leaders to insecure followers.

I believe that everyone faces this at different points in life. We all want to have good relationships with people so we can have influence. We gain the ability to effect change in others by influence. Without good relationships, we cannot effectively influence others. While this can be acknowledged as true, where do relationships originate? It is God that sets things in order. He ordains relationships and gives influence, and He is faithful to maintain them. We are responsible to love God and love one another selflessly. We cannot allow ourselves to be so taken up with the desire of trying to please and win others over that we end up receiving our affirmation and identity from them. We need to be those who run forward after what God has set in front of us, knowing that it is God who ordains the other pieces in our lives.

We are called to maintain peace with others as much as it concerns us. I believe this is possible without crossing the line of becoming people pleasers. We will always have three types of people in our lives:

1. People who receive our attempts to have relationship with them
2. People who are indifferent and don't mind knowing us or not
3. People who no matter what we do will be critical and hard to relate with

We must pursue peace and relationship with as many as we can. We need to ensure that we handle hard things along the way with humility. We should always seek to see that people around us are growing and finding their identities in the Lord. Just because someone doesn't like us doesn't mean that there is something we need to change. It may be something that they need to change. We should never fail to look at our lives and change anything the Lord speaks to us, but just because someone comes with a frustration does not mean we need to have a complete identity change. We need to walk confidently in who God made us and trust the Lord to help us even when others attempt to speak negatively about the things God is working inside of us.

> Bless those who persecute you; bless and do not curse. Rejoice with those who rejoice, and weep with those who weep. Be of the same mind toward one another. Do not set your mind on high things, but associate with the humble. Do not be wise in your own opinion. Repay no one evil for evil. Have regard for good things in the sight of all men. If it is possible, as much as depends on you, live peaceably with all men. Beloved, do not avenge yourselves, but rather give place to wrath; for it is written, "Vengeance is Mine, I will repay," says the Lord. (Rom. 12:14–19, NKJV)

Simon to Peter

Simon began to follow Jesus and do all that was asked of him. Whether he was aware of it or not, his identity was changing into the person Christ had called him to be. Day by day, he found himself further away from the original person who first met Christ on the shores of the Sea of Galilee.

One day on this new path of discovery with Jesus, Simon found himself face-to-face with a question he hadn't expected. "Who do you say that I am?" (Matt. 16:15) I wonder what thoughts flooded Simon's mind? It may have seemed like a silly question to ask, but the answer is one of the most important on earth. Who is Jesus to you?

Our identity is founded in the revelation of who Jesus Christ is to us personally. Peter's answer declared the divinity of Christ; he wasn't just another man or a prophet. He truly was and is the Son of God and the Savior of the world. This revelation meant that Simon's life was no longer his own; he was now a follower of the one who gave him life. Jesus declared that God the Father had revealed this to Simon, and then Jesus uttered something amazing to Simon. Jesus called him Peter. Peter, a rock.

Simon's identity was not only changed as a result of his actions, but now even what others called him reflected the fact that he had encountered Jesus. His revelation of Christ was where his newfound identity was confirmed. When we encounter Jesus and truly discover who He is, we will find who we are!

Simon started out on the right path. He responded to Christ's call and left all to follow Him. Now he found himself with a new name. He looked into the face of the king and was being transformed into the image he saw looking back at him. On a daily basis, he went back to the same place the change had started and sought for more. He talked to Jesus and allowed His words to change his heart, thoughts, and actions. Then one day, this very identity was called into question and tested.

I am tested daily while working with young people. The things I proclaim during youth services and leaders meetings are always tried and questioned. I love teaching others the importance of receiving correction and remaining moldable and humble before others. A young person can come into my office and say things that make me face some of the very things I have been teaching: "You could be a better youth pastor if you just…" or "Our services just aren't exciting like they used to be…" or "The last youth pastor used to…"

I'm tested in these situations.

Suddenly my God-given identity of being teachable and open to learning is put through the fire to see what comes out the other side. Believe me, I don't pass this test every time. Sometimes pride sneaks out, and I try to prove just how great I am and how little the other person knows. After an epic failure like this, I have to find the other person, humble myself, and apologize. When I fail in these tests, I feel like hiding in a hole. At this point, the enemy comes and whispers lies to me, "Maybe you are just faking all this leadership stuff, and you are not the man for the job." Simon was no different.

At the fire in the courtyard, a little girl could see that he looked like Jesus. His demeanor and speech mirrored that of the man being questioned by Pilate. Simon's identity was beginning to match that of Christ. The progress was evident. But Simon still did not have full confidence in his new identity. He doubted in his heart that change was actually taking place. The many words that tumbled out denied his identity to this simple onlooker.

In a moment of testing, Simon gave in and reverted back to the person he once was. Discouraged, he packed up and headed back to where he came from. It was much easier to hide behind the mask of a false identity that he was familiar with. The lying thoughts pounded in his head and told him that because he had failed this test, he had forfeited his whole new identity.

What Simon did not understand was that Jesus was still in hot pursuit!

> For it is God who works in you both to will and to do for His good pleasure. (Rom. 12:14–19, NKJV)

God not only gives us the new identity He wants us to walk in but helps us to walk in it. He knows that change is not easy. Even when we are like Simon and fall back into our old ways, God will tenaciously pursue us. He wants us to change and embrace the new identity more than we do. This persistent confidence is what we now can give to those we lead.

> We love Him because He first loved us. (1 John 4:19, NKJV)

I love rephrasing this verse as "We love others because He first loved us."

Simon went back to fishing. He found his old clothes, his old boat, and his nets. He was a natural leader, and his decision to revert back to the fishing lifestyle caused others to follow. He traded his new freedom and liberty for the familiar, even though it brought back the frustration of failing to catch fish! Simon thought the story of his life was completely written, but Jesus was just getting started.

Returning from another mundane day on the lake, Simon noticed someone standing on the shore. A voice called out, and immediately Simon remembered the first time he met Christ. "This is Jesus." But Simon still struggled to recognize that the call and new identity that Christ gave him was solid. It would continually propel him forward, not backward.

Simon scrambled to put on his tunic as he jumped into the water to swim to Jesus. He was too afraid to come as he was. He felt ashamed and endeavored to cover his shortcomings and approach Jesus in a state of being put together. The problem was that the only way he knew to appear back together was reminiscent of the past.

Simon redressed himself in his old identity and swam to shore.

Simon backslid, denied Jesus, and returned to everything that Jesus had pulled him from. Jesus had every right to rebuke him and show him just how wrong he was. If it had been me, I know I would have. I have, at times, done that to those I lead. But Jesus did not do that. He asked Simon to bring him some fish and then made him breakfast. I strongly believe that eating together is a spiritual thing, and this story proves it! (All the food lovers said, "Amen.") As they finished breakfast, Jesus asked Peter three times, "Do you love me?" Through this interchange, Jesus showed Peter that he was forgiven fully, and his identity remained intact. Christ desired to solidify in Peter's mind the relationship of love that existed between them. This was the basis of an accurate self-identity for Peter.

His God-given identity was renewed through the power of forgiveness for his great failure. Once again, Jesus uttered those familiar words to Peter, "Follow me." Everything starts and ends in the same place—follow the Lord, and let him define who you are.

Jesus originally called Simon a rock based on his newfound revelation of who Jesus was. Now Jesus reaffirmed who Peter was—one called to follow Him all the way!

When failure isn't dealt with God's way, insecurity tries to sneak in, and the only answer is to put God back in His rightful place. We must remind ourselves who Jesus really is and who we are in light of that understanding. Insecurity is a form of pride that can destroy a leader. When we think that we are not good enough, we allow a fear to overshadow the change that God began in us. We take control back from God and try to do things by ourselves. The only way to overcome this is to place our eyes back on Christ and allow Him to put us back in our rightful place. We are His servants. When He is on the throne of our lives, we live differently, and see ourselves differently. Insecurity has no place when we are fixated on the face of Jesus, and are assured by what is reflected back…our identity in Christ.

Our journey toward this God-centered identity is different from that of others. Most of us aren't fishermen! We may feel alone in the things that the Lord is asking us to do. The identity God is giving us may make us stand out a bit from others. Many of us shy away from anything that brings attention or makes us different. What if I told you that being unique is not a negative byproduct of change but the very thing God created us to be?

5

UNIQUE AS ONLY YOU CAN BE

Young people today are stuck in a deadly cycle when it comes to identity. A majority of the most famous people in our culture today are some of the unhappiest and unhealthy people. They struggle with addictions, broken families, and (most amazingly) identity problems. We have an entire generation of young people trying to pattern their lives after some of the most unhappy and unfulfilled people in our culture. They are imitating and building their identity from others who haven't even found theirs. It is just like the enemy to do such a thing: to glamorize unhappiness and make it appealing to those who are already happy. Identity is not simply a word thrown around. It is a matter of life and death.

> The thief does not come except to steal, and to kill, and to destroy. I have come that they may have life, and that they may have it more abundantly. (John 10:10, NKJV)

When it comes to identity we tend to have a copy-and-paste mentality. We think the answer is to find someone who acts the way that we want to act and simply copy this trait and paste it into ours. We do this with dress, the way we talk, the things we listen to, and just about every other area. We find the particular thing we like and then copy and paste. The problem is, true identity is rooted in our life experiences. God has designed us all, and He makes us into the people we are to be. Copying and pasting has no foundation in anything other than carnal vanity.

I have been taking some Bible college courses lately, and it is a surreal experience to be back in school again. I have homework, tests, and critiques of my work. Worst of all, I am paying for it. I also have to write many papers. In the guidelines for the school, it is mentioned that plagiarism will not be tolerated. Nobody appreciates copied things especially if the writer claims it as their own. Plagiarism is taking something that someone has made and trying to convince others that it is your own. This is exactly what we do with our identities. We take parts of other people's lives and try to force them to fit into ours. We are plagiarizing people's identities and are left wondering why they do not fit right into ours. We get stuck in this cycle of copying and pasting, and when it doesn't work, we find someone else to copy. There must be a better way.

When I was first dating my wife, she asked me what my favorite thing about her was. I confidently responded without a second thought that I liked the fact that she was unique. Her response was not what I was expecting. I expected her to blush and be flattered, but the response I got was almost like she was offended. She continued to explain to me that when she thought of unique, she thought of the awkward person in school or the puppy that didn't fit into the litter. She felt like it was the thing parents said about a child at playgroup who was weird but needed to be referred to in a nicer way. Our definitions of unique were extremely different. I explained that when I thought of unique, I thought of something that was one-of-a-kind. A prized possession that people would pay insane amounts of money for because it was nothing like the rest. A trait that shouldn't be avoided, but sought after. What makes some of the most collectible things have value is the fact that they are unique, one-of-a-kind items. After this explanation, I got the expected response: blushing and smiles.

Uniqueness is something that is criticized in our culture, but deep down I believe it is quietly sought after. Everyone wants to be their own person and have people accept them as themselves. I believe that the hidden secret of uniqueness is the fact that it is not simply copied and pasted from somewhere else. It is created and owned solely by the individual person. I believe true God-birthed identity is not a random combination of other people's identities but an individualized, unique creation. He forms each person like a work of art. Starting with a blank canvas, He creates something new, exactly according to His plan and purpose for that person. One of the names for God is Creator. He loves doing this, and I believe He has taken the time to create each one of us uniquely.

Ever since I was young, I have always been a bit odd. It may be because I live in between two cultures or the fact that I have had so many unique experiences while growing up. Whatever the cause, I have always been a little different than those around me. I never quite understood why and even tried at times to be less different. I remember the first time that someone called me out and said, "Seth, you are bit strange, but I like it." They explained that the fact that I wasn't like everyone else challenged them to be okay with being different. It wasn't until I moved to Uganda and began to walk in the things that God called me to that my differentness started to make sense. I fit in perfectly here. Our identity will always line up with the call of God on our life. We may look a little out of place on our way there, but that is because we weren't made for where we are now. We were created with a purpose in mind.

Recently, a good friend passed away, and it shook me up. He was too young, and still had so much that God was using him for. He was a missionary church planter, who was doing an awesome job. He was one of the most generous people I have met. "Missionary" and "generous giver" usually do not go together. Generally missionaries are the ones asking for funds, not the ones giving. He was a little different. He gave so much, and the testimonies shared after he passed told stories of how generous he was. Beyond his great ministry impact, the thing that I like the most about him was the fact that he was unique like me. He was a little awkward and didn't really fit in anywhere. He talked half American English and half Japanese English. The best part was that he didn't care. He simply was following the call of God on his life, and people noticed. He was confident in his God-given identity and where it had taken him.

Accepting your uniqueness is being confident in who God made you to be, even when you don't fit the mold set by others around you. Some may try to copy and paste uniqueness. They try to be different for the sake of being different. They cross into the realm of weird and even become proud of how different they are. This isn't what I am talking about. Godly identity that is different than those around is one that is received and walked out in humility, knowing that it is God who birthed it. It is simply walking in the things of God and not even noticing (or at least not caring) that you are a bit odd. I believe uniqueness like this is normal in the lives of those who have found their God-given identity.

As leaders we need to understand that people are watching our lives while trying to figure out theirs. They are looking at us not as people who have arrived but as those who are a few steps farther along than them. Many have questions, and even though they may be afraid to ask, they are looking for the answers through watching how we live in every situation. I always find leaders who are a little quirky and confident in their uniqueness to be more approachable than those who have it all together. Looking like you are supposed to and being polished isn't something I necessarily look up to. As we walk confidently in our uniqueness, I think we will unconsciously encourage others to do the same, and they will seek counsel in how to find their identity. Being real and living with honesty opens the door for relationship. When others see us simply trying to follow the Lord, we will inspire them to begin their walk on this journey toward a unique, God-initiated identity.

> Before I formed you in the womb I knew you. (Jer. 1:5, NKJV)

> For You formed my inward parts; You covered me in my mother's womb. I will praise You, for I am fearfully and wonderfully made. (Ps. 139:13–14, NKJV)

I believe we hurt God's heart when we try to be anything different than what He made us to be. It is like us telling Him that we are better than

Him at deciding who we should be and how we should look. The time, effort, and love He poured into each one of us is something we will be accountable for. Will we fight our entire lives trying to be something different, or will we joyfully accept and walk in the fullness of what the God created in us?

The only way we can walk this out correctly is ensuring that we are walking this path with God Himself. We can't understand Him or any part of life if we don't really know Him for ourselves. One of the key foundations for our identity with Jesus is recognizing who we are to Him. Are we basing who we are on things we have heard about Jesus from a third party or are we building with the very Word of God spoken to us directly from Christ Himself?

6

ENSURING WE ARE DISCIPLES

And Jesus came and spoke to them, saying, "All authority has been given to Me in heaven and on earth. Go therefore and make disciples of all the nations, baptizing them in the name of the Father and of the Son and of the Holy Spirit, teaching them to observe all things that I have commanded you; and lo, I am with you always, even to the end of the age." Amen.

—Matthew 28:18–20, NKJV

God encouraged His most trusted followers to live their lives in such a way that in one aspect it was contrary to those around, and in another, exactly the same. The basis for their lifestyle was a personal relationship with Jesus Christ Himself. Then, out of that relationship flowed a desire to help others find the same place they had reached. This was the fruit of their overwhelming personal need for their newfound relationship with Christ. It was more than a quiet, pious faith that caused this to be replicated in others but a divine conviction that moved them to action.

They heeded the command to "go." This was initiated by what they had tasted and seen in their own lives. They truly had found The Way (the earliest followers of Christ were called those of the way). There was a supernatural understanding of "both/and" in all that they did. None were complacent enough to fall on one side of an issue and become part of the general voice (either option A or B). They looked at all things circumspectly, motivated by love and unity, and put effort in becoming more like Christ (the one they knew). They helped others to find Him as the culmination of any form of interaction. They looked at the same problem, the same text, the same situation, and found a new solution based on age-old Biblical truth. To the amazement of onlookers, they did the same as their master. Everyone who interacted with them saw a difference and testified "these have been with Jesus" (Acts 4:13). They did not want to be the loudest voice in the room, the most educated, or best looking; they wanted people to meet and see Christ for who He really was. The most effective way to do that was to ensure they were continually being transformed to look like Him and were helping others to do the same. They were disciples that made disciples. They were people who had found their identity in Jesus and desperately wanted others to find theirs as well.

Christ never allowed them to become followers that simply followed. In the New Testament, there were two groups of people who sought after the Christ. There were the crowds that consisted of everyone—sometimes thousands and sometimes hundreds who crowded around to see Jesus. These crowds comprised those people who came for a while, never accepted any personal responsibility, and often left...sometimes in huge numbers (John 6:60, Matt. 22:22). Then there was a group, separate from the crowd: the disciples! The disciples were once part of the crowd, but what set them apart from the rest was that they also did the things that Jesus did. Christ put the most of His effort, time, and resources into making twelve disciples. These twelve eventually went out and turned the world upside down. If Christ did this in His lifetime, surely His disciples would do the same in theirs and this would repeat itself in each generation. A disciple is one who makes disciples. Simon Peter had to constantly battle with this question. Am I simply part of the crowd, or am I a disciple?

Being personally discipled by the Lord is what will continue to sustain our lives as ministers through the years. I have seen so many fiery leaders that have enough passion and drive to literally impact any area they would want to touch. For many of them this fruitful season was short-lived. They were here, and then they were gone. They started in the right way, but along the way, they forgot the fundamental truths that made them fruitful in the first place. To them, being a disciple was simply a step to becoming some other thing instead of it being their foundation. Being a disciple first and everything else second simply became a great idea that they taught but did not actually live. Without noticing, they went from being a disciple to following a prevalent crowd. They became a leader following other leaders, and not Christ. These once-grounded disciples abdicated the responsibility of "chief discipler" to popularity and relevancy. In order for us to make disciples, we need to ensure that we are always disciples first. Being a disciple is not simply a step to finding our identity. It is and always will be our identity.

The Crowd

> During those days another large crowd gathered. Since they had nothing to eat, Jesus called his disciples to him and said, "I have compassion for these people; they have already been with me three days and have nothing to eat. If I send them home hungry, they will collapse on the way, because some of them have come a long distance." (Mark 8:1–3, NIV)

Characteristics of the crowd are as follows:

- Usually big numbers
- Gathered when Jesus was near
- Generally came together when something miraculous was done
- Never came prepared (needed food, clothing, etc.)
- Often left or were sent away after the teaching
- Easily swayed by others
- Sought what was popular

The crowds that we see around Jesus often came because of what they had heard about Him. Some came just to see why others were gathering. I live in a culture with a lot of similarities to that of the Bible (Uganda). Whenever something happens like a car accident or a fight, crowds quickly form and seem like they come out of almost nowhere. None plan to be there, they just are. Sometimes the crowd is so big that you can't see what they are actually gathering about. The report plays like a game of telephone from those in front to those on the fringes. Each word is coated with the vessel's own opinion. It is very easy for the crowd to be swayed based on what the majority thinks, even if it is wrong, or goes against an individual's thoughts or morals. When you are in the crowd, it is so easy to be enveloped in what the rest think. Once the moment is over and the crowd disperses, so does your involvement. You go about life waiting for the next gathering of the crowd. You do not have any convictions of your own and do not take any ownership for the reason the crowd gathered. This is proven when the police show up. Within an instant, there is no one to be seen. The moment a hard thing happens, or the depth of the root is tested, the internal urge to flee is satisfied. Biblically speaking, the crowd represents those who add their voice to the roar of the culture and never speak for themselves. They cannot explain to anyone else the reason for their convictions because they have personally only gone as far as the crowd has. Their attempt at discipleship is ineffective because they have not allowed themselves to become, or remain, disciples. Words simply heard from a third party will never be effectively imparted to another with the same authority, or conviction, as the one who originally heard it, and certainly not as much as the one who spoke it. If we are part of the crowd, then all we know is what others have told us. Our very speech will be ineffective, and we will find a lack of fruit in our lives. We will doubt the things we have heard and ultimately, like everyone else in the crowd, we will turn back when the meeting is over and return to our normal business. We will not only be failing to fulfill the great commission but will be perpetually making other crowd followers. A crowd follower making other crowd followers is not a disciple.

The Disciples

> Then Jesus said to the twelve, "Do you also want to go away?" But Simon Peter answered Him, "Lord, to whom shall we go? You have the words of eternal life. Also we have come to believe and know that You are the Christ, the Son of the living God." (John 6:67–69, NKJV)

Characteristics of the disciples are as follows:

- Committed
- Did not come early or leave late—they simply never left
- Were sent to do the same things as Christ
- Bore fruit everywhere they went
- Taught others to do the same as they did
- Fought for their beliefs
- Oftentimes looked different than the norm

The disciples that followed Christ were unique. They were committed and resolute in their conscious pursuit of Him. These were the ones that heard the call of Christ themselves. The foundation of their relationship was not based on a general response, or blanket confession of being a Christian. For each one of them there was a distinct moment when Jesus came to where they were and said, "Follow Me." They personally heard the call from their Savior, and their response was none other than to obediently follow and do what He commanded them to do. They understood that everything Christ did was modeling for them the very things they were to do when He left. It was never meant to be a sit-and-watch relationship. That is what the crowds did. For the disciples they were sitting, learning, and then going out and implementing in one fluid motion. Some did this full-time, while others worked a regular job as well as did Paul when he worked as a tentmaker. These disciples were always students themselves, and as they were faithful in the classroom, they were also faithful in their homework. Their passing mark was that they went out and made disciples of all nations.

There is a contradiction I see in many Christians and leaders. They truly love God in principle, they say they are Christians, and they do many of the actions that other Christians do. They may have fallen in love with God for a season, but sadly, they do not have a life-giving and life-changing relationship with Him. They are not motivated to the extent that they go out and lead others into a dynamic relationship like they have. Maybe this lack of obedience is motivated by fear or lack of teaching? But for some, maybe they never truly experienced a personal moment when the Lord called them by name. They never knew that Christ called them to be a disciple, not just part of the crowd. They never understood that their love relationship with Christ, not religious duty, would motivate them to make disciples. Unfortunately, they don't realize that the true measure of a fruitful life is the ability to make other disciples. We need to return and teach this generation to follow Christ's model and the one preached by His disciples: become disciples that go and make disciples.

Walking as a disciple who makes disciples

I believe this is one of the most important parts of finding our identity: learning how to walk both as a disciple and as a disciple maker. This takes a life-long preparation that must start early in a young person's life and in our lives as leaders. I would say that this process is a prerequisite to being called a disciple. You can't lead a generation to life without being simply that…alive!

I believe Jesus left for us an attainable example set forth by His life and recorded in the Bible. I want us to look at a couple of prerequisites that are important before and throughout this process:

1. Jesus was in preparation for thirty years before He stepped out in public ministry and started making disciples. He learned, was tested, and empowered by the Holy Spirit before He made any attempt to make disciples.

One amazing thing that happens during discipleship is impartation. Impartation is the transfer of you (something more than just words) to another person. The Bible says, "For out of the abundance of the heart the mouth speaks" (Matt. 12:34). Impartation is the transfer of heart. I have watched people I am working with begin to imitate some of the worst parts of me. I never spoke of these things, but they were certainly part of me, and others began to emulate them. As I make disciples, I need to ensure that I am allowing myself to be tested, challenged, taught, and empowered by the Holy Spirit. If I am not being first discipled by the Lord, I will not make disciples the way that Christ did.

> Imitate me, just as I also imitate Christ. (1 Cor. 11:1, NKJV)

2. John the Baptist did the work of God by laying the path before Christ began His ministry. Jesus publicly honored John for all he did. As we attempt to find our identities today, we must honor those who went before us and taught us how. We are not starting from scratch but continuing something that has already been started!

When God called Moses He declared Himself, "I am the God of your father—the God of Abraham, the God of Isaac, and the God of Jacob" (Exod. 3:6, NKJV). He ensured that Moses understood that he was being called in the context of generations. I think it is so easy to discredit those who have gone before us in our attempt to show the need for change. The model we follow should give honor and bring change by building on the foundation laid, and not feeling the need to first tear down and start from scratch. I am in ministry today because of those who went before me. They started a great work that I get the opportunity to continue, knowing that someone else will take it from me in the future. The names of those who laid the foundation may be unknown to many, but I want those I lead to know their names and understand that we are part of something so much bigger and enduring than us. I want part of my identity to be that I always acknowledge those who went before us.

> Give to everyone what you owe them: If you owe taxes,
> pay taxes; if revenue, then revenue; if respect, then respect;
> if honor, then honor. (Rom. 13:7, NKJV)

Part of being a disciple is humility. My humility is tested when I am tempted to take credit for things that I did not do. Humility gives honor to others and especially those who have had a notable impact in my life. My identity will always include pieces of those who have poured into me. That is okay. God brought them into my life for a purpose. I may pray like my mentor, or study like I was taught in Bible school. Praise the Lord for Godly models and impartation from others. We need God to help us glean the good from leaders and leave the bad. We should always welcome God to be the primary one that is pouring into us, but we should also allow Him to use others along the way. Uniqueness, when molded by godly models and filtered through God's Word will produce godly identity in us as disciples. That will stand the test of time.

As we continue to be disciples who follow Christ, we will always have those around us who don't want us to change or don't believe that we can change. Their motivation for this may be many different things. They may have tried before and failed. They may be part of the crowd and not a disciple. They may simply not want us to succeed. How do you change when others don't support you?

7

CHANGING WHEN OTHERS WANT TO KEEP YOU IN A BOX

Jesus said that prophets were without honor in their own hometown (Matt. 13:57). There could be many reasons for this statement, but I think one of the biggest reasons is that people are great at putting others in a box. A box made by the other person. A box made by past experiences. This isn't the kind of box you pack when you move! We might have changed, or want to change, but those around us try to keep us the same people who they know. This could be completely innocent on their part or potentially on purpose. If we do not recognize that this is happening, we could find ourselves not changing into the identity that the Lord has for us.

Our culture generally wants us to fit into its mold. This can affect us personally. We feel justified in our actions when we see others doing the same. We pressure others to do things the way we do to justify our pursuits. Individuality is honored when found, and even encouraged, but it is never accepted by those who deep down want to be normal as the culture surrounding them would define it. The honest truth is that we will never please everyone nor will we live up to his or her measure of success. The only one that we need to worry about pleasing is the Lord. As a leader this pressure is one that we need to stop trying to fix. Even if everyone around us wants us to be a certain way, speak a certain way, or dress a certain way, we must stand up and be the leader/pastor/person whom God wants us to be. It may be different, but I beg you to understand that our young people, and especially our culture needs new, unique, and fresh models of the gospel being lived out through our lives! Jesus modeled "different" for us:

> When Jesus had finished saying these things, the crowds were amazed at his teaching, for he taught with real authority—**quite unlike** their teachers of religious law. (Matt. 7:28–29, NLT, emphasis mine)

Discovering and exploring the sights and sounds of new places excites me. I love it! In these situations, I get to be whomever I want. The people I interact with have no idea who I am and will most likely never see me again. I feel free! If I want to be more outgoing than before, I can. If I want to be quiet, I can. Nobody knows the difference. Whenever we have short-term mission teams come to be with us, I tell them the same thing. Be free to step out in things you have never tried before. If you have never been bold, now is your chance. Step out in a complete newness, believing that when you go back, you will take your newfound identity with you.

People around us may think we are acting weird; they may question our motives and may even judge us for trying to change. But we need to step out and allow the Lord to change us no matter what. People will come around eventually if our motivation is truly from the Lord. The best part is that we will have given them confidence that if we can do it, so can they. Our obedience to the Lord will encourage others to also step out in obedience.

Peter was rash in his decisions. He was extremely emotional and was led by how he felt in the moment. All those around knew this about him. It was expected of him. In rashness he made huge promises to Jesus, not thinking about the consequences of his promises. Peter had boldly declared that even if he had to die with Jesus he would.

> Peter said to Him, "Even if I have to die with You, I will not deny You!" (Matt. 26:35, NKJV)

When the soldiers came to arrest Jesus in the Garden of Gethsemane, Peter and the other disciples were present. In an attempt to prove his loyalty to those around him, and to Jesus Himself, Peter drew his sword and cut off the ear of one of those coming to arrest Jesus. He was trying to live up to the standard he had declared to everyone else. The pressure to be something is so strong at times. I think there are two things that make changing into a new identity so hard.

1. Trying to prove that you have indeed changed to those looking on (Pleasing man)

Peter had a big battle in front of him. Not only was he trying to change more and more into the person Jesus wanted him to be, but he was also trying to prove to others around him that he had indeed changed. Peter had to fight against this feeling of needing to prove something to those around him. All of the disciples were working overtime to impress Jesus. We find them arguing over who was greater.

> Then a dispute arose among them as to which of them would be greatest. And Jesus, perceiving the thought of their heart, took a little child and set him by Him, and said to them, "Whoever receives this little child in My name receives Me; and whoever receives Me receives Him who sent Me. For he who is least among you all will be great." (Luke 9:46–48, NKJV)

Our world and culture tries to tell us that we need to strive to please the people around us. "You will get a promotion at work if you impress the boss." You will get a great opportunity to speak somewhere if you just impress the right person. If you simply show that you are better than someone else, you will advance. But striving to succeed will focus on pleasing people and that leads to some really ugly identity traits.

If people are the ones that we are trying to please, then when they don't give us the affirmation we are seeking, we are crushed. If people are the reason we are serving God, then when hard times come, we seek after people to fix it. Jesus, in His great wisdom, grabbed a child and explained that striving is not the answer. Humility and accepting that we are all children of God is our answer. There is nothing too small or insignificant for us to do because we are not serving man but God.

We can't allow other's view of us, or lack of acceptance, to stop us from changing into God's design for our lives. If we were becoming better people to please them, then their opinion would be the base line for our success. But when God is our motivation then no matter what others say, we can continue. God is the reason!

2. Fear

Working with and listening to young people, I hear over and over that one of the biggest hindrances to God moving in their lives is the four-lettered word…fear. Fear of being alone. Fear of the future. Fear of change. Fear of sin being exposed. Fear of the great unknown. Fear of never getting married. Fear of failing. Fear comes in many different forms, but is always fear! Fear has the ability to cripple even the bravest person. If fear is not dealt with, the transformation that Christ is working in us is hindered. Fear displaces the first ingredient for following Christ—faith. Faith has the ability to look fear in the face and say, "Be what it may, I will not stay captive to fear."

> For God has not given us a spirit of fear, but of power and
> of love and of a sound mind. (2 Tim. 1:7, NKJV)

God is not a God of fear but a God of faith!

Throughout the entirety of Jesus and Simon's relationship, we see God working faith into his life by confronting fear. Many of these lessons were taught on the Sea of Galilee. Remember this is the sea that was sustained by the hand of God. To fish on this lake required faith that God was keeping the salt inflow from overpowering the fresh water. Here, Simon began to find out who he truly was. Change is possible, but often times it requires confronting the things that frighten us the most. Identity is found in the place where there is no fear…right next to Jesus.

As leaders of young people, we often try new things. Every area of ministry is and should be in a constant state of newness. Young people have an uncanny ability to sense monotony and run from it. I am always scared when I step out to try something new—something I haven't done before. It is one thing to continue in things that have already been done and continue to renew them and make them better. Doing something that has never been done before when all eyes are on you is a different kind of monster. I fear failure. We will talk about how to deal with failure in the next chapter, but what about the fear of failing?

During this past season, I have been sensing the need to "graduate" some of our older leaders out of the youth ministry and propel them into a new season. We always need to make room for new, upcoming leaders on the decision-making team. These leaders have been the lifeblood of our ministry for many years now. They know how I think. They are strong leaders, and they have been tested. They do the things we are currently doing perfectly. That is the problem though. They are great at doing what we are doing but have lost that spark for thinking of new things to do. We are entering into a season where we are going to graduate these older ones and give them a new area of responsibility. In doing this, we may lose some of the "perfectness" in the current things we do, but we'll also gain an ability to think of new things with a new team. This scares me. What if we take too big of a step back? What if we regret this decision? What if...?

Sometimes fear can keep us from acting in faith. Instead of being a person of faith, we become a person of fear. Our identity is at risk if we allow fear to be a deciding factor in the things that we do. God works supernaturally in our places of uncertainty. This is where relying on His Word needs to outweigh the current landscape. All of our identities and gifts are different, but one thing must be a common factor. We are called to be people and leaders of faith. When fear presents itself, we should run headlong into it.

When I was younger, I was afraid of the dark. We have all had that feeling where the lights are off in a room, and we want to run away to a room with more light. When I got saved, fear was a big area of my life that God worked on. One of the things He challenged me to do was never allow fear to be my motivation for a decision. I took that to heart and have tried my best to apply it. Now, when I step into a dark room and everything inside of me wants to run away, I will stay standing in that room just to prove to myself that fear will not have an influence in my life.

Changing and growing even if people still have you in a box is a scary thing. As leaders who are seeking to walk in a new identity, we need to develop a tenacity to step out in faith and change as the Lord leads us. This may require changing our thoughts and actions, changing our surroundings, or even changing the things we are involved in. One of my favorite verses supports this…we must continually change and grow.

> But we all, with unveiled face, beholding as in a mirror the glory of the Lord, are being transformed into the same image from glory to glory, just as by the Spirit of the Lord. (2 Cor. 3:18, NKJV)

Faith to change is found in the face of our Savior. Sometimes the hardest thing to do is acknowledge this truth. Our favorite disciple was in a boat, but this time with the physical Jesus. (Matt. 8:26) Think about it. What could be more faith inspiring than being inches away from God incarnate? I have been afraid many times, but in my small frame of reference, I think that being next to the one who could sneeze and blow a hole in the earth would be a time that I would have confidence that everything would be okay. We must recognize that growing in faith doesn't happen automatically. It is something that has to be walked out.

Peter and the disciples were in a boat on the lake when a storm blew in. They were certain they were going to die. In panic, they turned to Christ who was peacefully asleep at the back of the boat. Frantically they detailed their current predicament to Him and how they were sure they were seconds away from meeting Him in a different context (eternity). Jesus simply stood up, and with a breath, calmed the storm and rebuked their lack of faith. He didn't rebuke them for not possessing the same amount of faith as Him but for losing the amount that they had already attained from following Him. They still had not learned how to walk in this newness that Jesus wished to solidify inside of them.

As we step out in the new identity Christ is working in us, we need to keep looking at Him as our benchmark. He is the one working it to fulfillment in us. When the storms arise around us (as they are promised to continue to do), we must not lose faith and revert to who we once were. We need to simply look into the face of Jesus. We must realign our faith in Him, turn from fear, and walk straight into the identity He has made for us!

The truth is that some people will be harder to convince than others as you change to be more like Christ. The only way I know how to change other people's thoughts about you is to love unconditionally and never stop being real in the process. What will help us break the box that others have put us in?

3. Genuineness

Being real is a difficult task as a leader. My wife is better at this than I am. She says and reveals things at times that make me cringe a bit when they are said in the company of others. Afterward, I am always thankful, when I see the result in the person we are talking to, when they also become brutally honest. People watching us are thankful for the anointing on our lives, and they want us to be people they can look up to. However, they also want us to be people they can relate to. When they see that we too are genuinely growing and changing, our impact is enlarged. There is no longer a wall between us. We have escaped the box they put us in!

When I first moved to Uganda, I was very different than I am today. I had been saved for three and a half years and had even been involved in leadership to some extent in my old youth group. In moving to Uganda, I was immediately thrown into pastoral leadership. I was given responsibility over the entire A/V team at the church and asked to help colead the first year of our young-adult internship. This was true baptism by fire. I discovered a problem during this season. I wasn't very good with people! I was more concerned about the success or right function of something than I was about the people involved. This led to a few tough years while I learned how to truly put people first.

Throughout this learning season, some people put me in this box. I heard many secret comments of how I could never change, and how I was terrible with people. For sure there were areas of weakness in me, but God was working on me and changing me. Truthfully, even after I knew that God had worked a huge transformation inside of me, others refused to acknowledge the growth. I was still in that box. At times I struggled, not knowing how to get them to see the change. Even though I had changed, they had not.

It was in this season that I began to be real with people. I confessed to them that I was still learning, and I admitted my shortcomings. I didn't hide the fact that God was changing me. As people saw my earnest and honest desire to change, they also saw that I was in fact changing. Their perspective also changed. I learned that genuineness isn't something that can be faked; it has to be just that—genuine.

4. Love

> And above all things have fervent love for one another, for "love will cover a multitude of sins." (1 Pet. 4:8, NKJV)

Along with genuineness, I believe that, love can tear down just about any box that another person has put you in. I have seen people whom I thought were impossible be changed by my constant attempt to love and reach out to them.

People have an amazing ability to sense motives. It's as if they are intuitive fake detectors. Many times people have sensed whether I was spending time with them because I loved them, or if it was simply pretense. I have had situations and relationships turn negative simply because I wasn't acting out of love. When we walk in our new identity and we seek to love the most difficult people, we will not only experience God's changing grace in us but in those around us as well.

Even when people are hard to convince that we have escaped the box, we need to know that God is fighting for us. As long as we are constant in our pursuit of loving others and being obedient to God, we will see seemingly hopeless relationships and our harshest critics eventually come around. Even if they don't, if love was our motive, we can keep a clean conscience before the Lord. Many times some of the hardest people to convince are also going through a difficult season of change themselves. It is my experience that one of two things will happen. They will either acknowledge their situation and apologize or a large issue of sin will be exposed in their life. If we have done all that we can on our side, and do not see a breakthrough, we have to remember that relationship is a two-sided thing. It may be that while God is working on us, He also needs to work on things in them as well. God is in control. Our top priority must be to keep our hearts right before Him.

People may look at us as still in that box, but Jesus will see us as the person He is forming us into. Others may call us Simon, but He calls us Peter! The problem is that sometimes Peter sill acted like Simon. Failure can try to permanently revert us back to the person we once were, to our old identity. Failing is part of life and one that is often the hardest. God is so amazing that He sees past even our biggest failures toward the person whom He has been creating in us from the beginning.

8

DEALING WITH FAILURE

I do not do extremely well when I try to do something and the result is not what I was hoping for. It is easy for me to get discouraged and almost depressed. When I was growing up, I did not have a father or a very tight-knit family. When I got saved, I realized that my background made me vulnerable. I searched for approval from adults, friends, parent figures, and anyone I had a relationship with. I put so much faith in these relationships that I would do anything I could to create them and maintain them. I found myself changing to be accepted or relatable to those I was with. I was constantly trying to change and fit in. When I failed at something, I felt like these relationships were in jeopardy. I tried to please everyone, and in my mind failure was not allowed. This self-imposed weight led to an incredible fear of failure in me. I lived in a state of anxiety, trying not to fail anyone, and this often actually made me fail at other things.

Peter struggled with the same issue. What about you?

Imagine Peter finally getting his footing in the things Jesus had continually spoken over him. Jesus, the ultimate encourager, had finally convinced Peter that he was something more than what he saw when he looked in the mirror. Peter was walking in them and even believing that this new identity was truly his. But time after time, the biggest discouragement would come again—failure. Even though his earnest effort was toward the opposite (success), he found himself coming to terms with the fact that instead of success, he had indeed failed.

One of the main reasons for pastors to leave the ministry is discouragement, often motivated by failure. Failure, whether big or small, whether others know or only I perceive it, is so discouraging! Every sense of making progress immediately comes crashing down, and an overwhelming feeling of stagnation fills our mind. Failure can be so all-consuming at times that even the most recent good fruit can look negative. This feeling, if not dealt with correctly, allows lies from the enemy to be believed as truth.

Peter had to deal with this sense of losing a battle he was fighting so hard to win throughout his walk with the Lord. Each time we lose a battle, it teaches us how God, the one who called us in the midst of our failures, wants us to deal with these very real issues.

Swimming instead of walking
One of the most notable of Peter's failures happened on the Sea of Galilee. Jesus sent His disciples ahead of Him to the other side of the lake. Jesus often left His disciples alone to give them a chance to break out of the nest a bit and test the things they were learning from Him. Frequently, it ended by Jesus having to intervene and set things right...another teaching opportunity. In Matthew 14:22, we find the disciples in the middle of the lake on their way to the other side. One of them, while keeping watch, noticed something that did not look like waves on the horizon. His first conclusion was that it must be a ghost, and internally his heart began to quicken its pace. Waking the other disciples, he shared his conclusion, and together they cried out in fear that a ghost was present. (Picture grown men in a boat screaming and holding onto each other.) These were the same disciples that just hours earlier were with the King of the Universe. When testing came, fear took over. Instead of faith, a sense of hopelessness entered in. Fear has the ability to completely take over a situation and make everything prior to that moment to be forgotten. Faith, on the other hand, is not concerned by the perceived momentary reality but by the guaranteed eternal fact that Jesus is greater.

Jesus revealed Himself to them before things got too out of hand. Peter, most likely embarrassed, had an awakening. A moment of faith (after a moment of great fear) birthed inside of him, and he stood up and asked Jesus to call him to join Him on the water. Jesus called Peter out. Peter began to walk on the water like he saw Jesus doing. What a moment of great victory, conquering every law of nature! A certifiable miracle!

The greatest victories are sometimes followed by the greatest failures. Peter in his great faith moment was distracted by the wind, waves, and fear. Suddenly, the courageous water walker started to sink. Would he always be the drowning fisherman? Things compound so quickly in times of failure. For Peter it was no longer about not being able to walk on the water, but now it was to avoid drowning. Thoughts like "You will always be a failing fisherman" and "Imagine what people will say" flooded his mind, many distractions that could keep Peter from the real answer—he needed a savior once again.

Peter called out to Jesus, and He came to rescue him from his failure.

Soaking wet, Peter got back into the boat. All eyes were on him, the failed fisherman. Jesus addressed the reason for his failure—"You of little faith." If Peter was anything like me, he would've wanted to crawl into a hole and never come out. Everything seemed like it was over, and anything else simply looked impossible because of one moment of weakness. Peter probably wanted to get off the boat and return to a place where the only ones that could witness his failures were the fish he failed to catch. Jesus, in His great wisdom, modeled for His disciples one of the best ways to overcome failure.

Matthew records that immediately upon entering the boat, while their minds were jumping to all different conclusions, they reached the other side. Failure is part of life, and there is always a lesson to be learned through it. I once read a sign that said, "Did ya learn anything?" Failing without a lesson learned is failure. What was the lesson for Peter? In that instant, Peter needed to not be a slave to fear but to faith. He needed to keep his eyes on Jesus even when the wind and waves grew higher and higher. He needed to remain focused and not allow any distraction. Once the lesson was learned, Jesus moved him on. You can't stay in the place of failure. There has to be a moment when you get up, dry off, and continue going toward the things God has set before you.

Failure does not negate the fact that Jesus still has a plan, and there is still work to be done. After the rebuke, Jesus got back to work, and He called Peter to come with Him, not the next day or in the next season but after a blink of an eye. When they reached the other side, the entire village came out, and many sick were healed. Jesus and all His disciples, including Peter, went forward in faith and power. Failure can never be excused and should not be taken lightly, especially if sin is involved. With the help of the Lord, we should identify and repent of the sin. It is important that we find someone who we can talk to and become accountable to. We truly are stronger together. After dealing with it, I believe one of the keys to overcoming failure is getting back up and continuing. There is too much to be done to spend days sitting and recounting failures. People need to know about Jesus, and they see Him through us. What was meant to be a failure that would eliminate us can now be a testimony of faith when we get up and move forward in power.

> The godly may trip seven times, but they will get up again. But one disaster is enough to overthrow the wicked. (Prov. 24:16, NLT)

Receiving correction while trying to rebuke Jesus

Another one of Peter's great failures is found in Mark 8.

> And He began to teach them that the Son of Man must suffer many things, and be rejected by the elders and chief priests and scribes, and be killed, and after three days rise again. He spoke this word openly. Then Peter took Him aside and began to rebuke Him. But when He had turned around and looked at His disciples, He rebuked Peter, saying, "Get behind Me, Satan! For you are not mindful of the things of God, but the things of men." (Mark 8:31–33, NKJV)

There are a few things in life that one should never do. Rebuking or trying to correct Jesus is definitely one of them. Peter had allowed pride to sneak into his life. When we are successful at things, we can begin to think that it is because of something we have done. "Perhaps I have prayed enough, and that is why I am so anointed. Maybe because I was nice to the lady at the store, the Lord spoke to me in a new way this morning." Obedience is an incredibly important part of serving the Lord, but obedience never gives a reason to boast and is never an excuse to be proud. Peter thought he knew better than Jesus. He thought that perhaps if he adjusted Jesus a bit, Jesus would understand that willfully giving Himself to suffer was a bad idea. Peter began to think like Simon again. He forgot the purpose of Jesus's coming. Peter was so convinced that he was right that he pulled Jesus to the side and began to rebuke Him. Peter thought he knew better than Jesus!

After watching Peter crash and burn, Jesus gave a rebuke of His own. He compared Peter to the original one who thought he knew better than God. It was Satan who attempted to exalt himself. Jesus used this opportunity to train and remind the disciples that Peter was thinking like a man, not God.

I don't know if there could be a worse moment than the creator of the universe likening you to His mortal enemy. Peter failed. He did so in a pretty grand fashion. Sometimes after failing we are in need of correction. As leaders this is something that we can never get tired of. No matter how big or important we get, we can never stop receiving correction or learning from our mistakes. Peter had to receive correction in front of all his friends. He had to witness Jesus using this moment to teach everyone else something extremely important about following Him. We must deny ourselves. I myself wouldn't think there was any way I could recover from a failure of this magnitude, but Jesus knew just what Peter needed.

> Now after six days Jesus took Peter, James, and John, and led them up on a high mountain apart by themselves; and He was transfigured before them. His clothes became

> shining, exceedingly white, like snow, such as no launderer on earth can whiten them. (Mark 9:2–3, NKJV)

Shortly after Peter's failure, Jesus revealed Himself in a fresh way. After failing, we often need to see Jesus in a new way, to be reaffirmed in His love and belief in us. The best thing we can do after falling short of what God has for us is not to run from Him, but straight toward Him. We need to see Jesus in a new way, to have a fresh revelation of who He is.

It is so interesting how we sometimes put ourselves in situations that God never intended for us. We think that since we are a leader, or a pastor, we are now either exempt from failing or not allowed to. This potentially leads us to cover up the areas where we could really use a fresh touch of God. Instead, we need to learn how to run to God and allow Him to reveal new levels of Himself. If we are not open before God, we won't be open to people. If we are not open to people, they won't be open to us and will continue to struggle silently. Our honesty about failure breeds more honesty.

I wish I could say that there was a guaranteed way to never fail again, but I know that failure is part of life. I pray that we can learn some lessons from Peter and his failures, knowing that we must individually learn to walk in the identity God made for us. Failures should never define us. Walking in our God-given identity is a daily learning process for each of us.

9

WALKING IN A NEW IDENTITY

My wife and I are youth pastors at a church in Uganda, East Africa. Living and serving in a culture you were not born in while still being connected to your birth culture can be challenging. You find yourself striving to fit into the culture you are trying to reach, all the while realizing that you have to change a lot to achieve this goal: your speech, dress, likes and interests, and even your response to conflict. In the years I have been here, I have been able to make great strides in my connecting to my new culture, but I realize I have a long way to go. Every once in a while, we have a team come from the United States, or we go back to visit. And I quickly learn that in my attempt to become more Ugandan, I have lost some of my natural ability to relate to US culture. I've struggled to know who I am at times. I now don't fit in 100 percent in either culture. I find myself in the midst of continual identity change based on where I am and to whom I am talking. "Why is your accent so funny?" I can get so lost in the mechanics of culture and identity that I lose my identity altogether. I am called to love God, love my wife, love people, and build the church. I can do this no matter where I am as long as I root my identity in the Lord and step out as a child of God daily. I wouldn't be honest if I didn't say that it is and will probably remain a constant struggle.

Jesus declared Simon to be Peter. Jesus had done His part as the ultimate identity giver. Peter was now divinely given a new identity. Soon after this experience with Christ on the shore of Galilee, Jesus left, and the new Peter had to learn to walk in this newness. It is easy to maintain a certain level of yourself when different people are around. I can be a sports fanatic when I am around sports fans, or a book junkie around people who enjoy reading, a Ugandan around Ugandans, an American around Americans, but when everyone leaves, I am left with the person whom I truly am. Peter walked as Peter when Christ was around, but when Jesus ascended to heaven, what was next?

An identity crisis generally comes my way when I am around strong leaders for the first time. I feel like I have to prove the strength of my leadership and end up making a fool of myself in the process. I am secretly afraid that I am not good enough and have to be something better than I actually am. I come back and realize that it ultimately doesn't matter what they think. I need to be what God has called me to be. Insecurity is the byproduct of an untested character trait in a person. What happens when no one is around, or in this case when someone is? Does your identity change depending on who is near, or who isn't? Our change-prone identity must to be rooted in the unchanging one.

I remember when I first got married to my beautiful wife. It was surreal. All of a sudden, I was married, and the person standing next to me was going to be by me for the rest of my life. We drove away from the church in her father's Mercedes convertible and all boundaries, time restrictions, and everything else was now gone. We were married. Over the next few weeks and months, it was a weird reality to fully embrace. I would be filling out a form and forget the fact that I was married. I would look down at the ring on my hand and be startled, even though I was legally married and all of my family and friends knew it. I had to learn how to walk in this new identity. There was nothing external that needed to change except for me to simply walk in this dream that had become my reality.

As leaders God has called us to be something great and has divinely placed us where we are currently. He has prepared us from before time to be the people who are needed to fulfill the call He placed on our lives.

Our ability to walk in this identity is vital, not just to our own success as His followers but for the success of the future call of those around us. The people we lead need us to be the people God made us to be, not those whom others think we should be. If Peter had remained as Simon, he would have never become the great apostle that touched the nations. He would have been the below-average fisherman named Simon. His fruit and legacy was rooted in His identity. Your effectiveness is tied to your ability to be who God made you to be.

I have a friend named Ben who tells a great story of when he first got married. Prior to meeting his beautiful wife the only thing he wore was Nike T-shirts, jogger pants, and Nike shoes. This was his style, and he was convinced he looked good. He landed the girl, so he assumed he was doing something right. Over time, his wife purchased for him an entire closet full of new clothes. They were stylish, and if he would ever wear them, he would discover how great he would look in them. The problem was he wasn't willing to put his new clothes on. More importantly he wasn't willing to take his old clothes off. In order to put his new identity on, he needed to take his old one off. He needed to let go of what he thought his look was and put on newness. What are some things that the Lord would ask you to take off in order to put on the new things God has for you?

How do we walk in newness of identity? (Humility)

Faith and humility are needed for God to continue working in our lives. I don't think we can ever have too much of these qualities. We have talked about faith, but humility is another key for continually walking in newness.

When I was younger, I used to spend every summer on my grandparents' grape farm in Northern California. I was allowed to drive a tractor when I was way too young. I remember the first time my grandfather asked me to disk the field for him. The field must be disked before it is watered. Disking softens the ground and prepares it to receive water and channel it to the grape vines. I was so excited I could hardly contain it. Grandpa took time to explain to me how to do it and that because I was new, I could not do it the way I saw him do it. His reason being that he had been farming for fifty-plus years and I obviously had not. He made me repeat back to him the fact that I could not turn down every row. I had to do every other row and then come back because I hadn't learned to turn the tractor sharp enough yet. I was so excited that I nodded my head and waited until he released me to go.

About an hour in to my task, I noticed that it was taking me twice as long as my grandfather. Pride snuck up in me. I had been doing this an entire hour already, and surely I was experienced enough to drive like my grandfather did. I told myself that at the next turn, I would simply whip into the next row and continue on. The turn fast approached, and I had convinced myself that it was going to be easy. I turned that wheel as hard as I could, and instead of going down the row, I started straight down the row of grapes. I destroyed several grape vines before I finally stopped. Sitting on top of the tractor, I realized I had a problem.

I had allowed pride to take me off the path. Not simply off the path, but I literally destroyed part of the crop. Pride takes us off the path that God has set in front of us and tries to convince us that there are shortcuts to the things of God. As leaders we must remain humble and obedient to the things the Lord tells us. Sometimes growth or change doesn't come as fast as we want it. We can be tempted to short-circuit the learning process. I wanted my grandfather's skill but didn't want to put in the time and effort to learn.

Walking in the new identity that God has for us will require us to remain in a place of humility and continual learning from God himself. Peter tried to short-circuit the plan of God by chopping off the ear of one of those who came to arrest Jesus. Peter was convinced that Jesus had waited long enough to take over the kingdom in natural terms. He didn't realize that Jesus was going to die on the cross, and the process was much different and longer than Peter could have ever imagined.

Often times the process that God uses to change us is much different than the way we would have done it. It is longer, harder, and costs more than we could ever think. I saw someone illustrate this during a sermon once. He drew an "A" and a "B"—the "A" being the starting point of the journey and the "B" being the ending point. Then he drew a line straight from point A to point B saying that this was our plan for life. Next, he proceeded to start at A and draw on every piece of the board including circles and swoops before ending at point B. He explained that this is God's way. The journey of the nation of Israel in the wilderness looked like this. From Egypt to the Promised Land should have only taken two weeks and was a relatively straight line. Looking at the way God took them is far from this ideal. God needed to change them into the people who would be able to fight and conquer the Promised Land.

Just because the process takes longer than we thought doesn't mean that God is delaying. The fact that God is taking longer to work His identity into us means that the person we will become will match the call that He has placed on our lives. The bigger the call, the bigger the character and identity God needs to work into us. Only humility can guard our hearts so that we can stay teachable and moldable throughout the process as God slowly reveals the future.

At times we may need to simply hold on! The good news is that we are holding on to the one who has never failed. He is unmovable and as we anchor our identity in Him, we will see all that He has for us come to pass.

> This hope we have as an anchor of the soul, both sure and steadfast, and which enters the Presence behind the veil.
> (Heb. 6:19, NKJV)

These are all things that we can begin to walk in today. We can start by seeking the Lord for ourselves and asking Him to reveal Himself to us. We can ask God to help us see ourselves through His lens, to literally have His mind when we think of ourselves. Walking starts when we choose to take the first step and then continue with another step after that. What is God's first step for you?

10

WHAT ABOUT YOU?

It is amazing that God has given all of us the power of free will—the ability to choose and make decisions for ourselves. God doesn't want a robotic people who worship Him out of obligation. He desires a people who freely choose Him. He wants us to see all that the world has to offer and still choose Him, knowing that He is faithful and will give us the desire of our hearts. This could be a negative or positive thing. If we desire sin, God will allow us to find it. I have seen many times in my own life a negative desire leading to a reality. I believe the amazing godly thing is that we also have the ability to choose righteousness and to walk in the identity God has shown us.

As we discuss some practical steps we can take to walk in all that God has for us, I felt compelled to preface my comments with this: *You must choose to walk in a new identity.*

Walking in newness of identity is something that can be read about, talked about, and even desired. If you are anything like me, something happens when the time comes to actually do it. I have had ideas and goals to change the world almost every morning while I stand in the shower. The problem is that when I step out of the shower and think of the work necessary to make my thoughts a reality, I simply leave them as a dream. Staying the same is so much easier; it is normal and the thing we are used to. We have done it for so long that changing even feels wrong at times. But just like Peter, even if we fail more times than we can count, the end result is worth the journey and the cost. God has put something great in front of each one of us, and each of us is the only person he designed and made to fulfill each puzzle-shaped hole. Our call and our identity are intrinsically linked. We will only discover one when we are actively pursuing both. We need to start by choosing to walk in newness no matter what.

So what next?

1. We must honestly look at ourselves in the mirror of the Lord.

> But we all, with unveiled face, beholding as in a mirror the glory of the Lord, are being transformed into the same image from glory to glory, just as by the Spirit of the Lord. (2 Cor. 3:18, NKJV)

I think it is important for us to understand who we are now. As much as God wants to change us daily to look more like Him, the process of change started a long time ago. It is impossible to be serving the Lord and remain the same. God has changed many things in each of us, and it is important to identify what God has done already. These may be permanent changes. I once smoked, and now I don't. They may be ongoing glory-to-glory changes. God has given me great freedom in the area of purity, and I'm praying for more and more. Like everything else when we come to God, we should start by thanking Him for how far He has brought us. Earlier in the book, I recommended using a starting point to measure progress. In simply looking back from the point when we first met Christ to where we are today, we can see many changes in our identity and reasons to thank the Lord.

As we look at ourselves with Christ as our filter, it is easy to see the things that He is and that we may not yet be. I know in my life I try to keep a running list of areas and identities that I am praying over and allowing the Lord to change. I list some of these here:

- Take away my pride, and give me humility.
- Take away any lust, and give me purity.
- Take away any selfishness, and give me selflessness.
- Forgive me for being unloving, and help me to love like You love.

Taking a moment and practically allowing God to show us the areas where He wants to reveal His identity in us is a great place to start. My prayer for myself is that this will be an ongoing thing until I die. I should continually allow God to have areas in me that He is working on.

We never reach a stopping point in changing to look more like the Lord. Sometimes it is others who show us areas we need to change. There are certain people who are great at bringing out ugly sides of me. Either they get on my nerves or they aren't afraid to tell me an area that I should work on. Other times the Lord will use particular situations to challenge me to look more like Him.

Years ago, as I was driving home from work, I passed by a park where homeless people gathered at night to sleep. I felt the Lord nudge me to stop and take some food to some of the people staying there. For many reasons, I convinced myself not to do that and proceeded home. While pouring myself a bowl of cereal, I couldn't take it anymore, so I got back in my car with some food and drove back to the park. I spent the next forty-five minutes wandering through the park looking for even one person. I could not find even one. The Lord challenged me in that moment that He didn't only want me to be a person who obeyed but one who obeyed instantly. That delayed obedience was in fact disobedience. He wanted to change my identity.

2. We need to ask ourselves what are the non-God things in our lives (not necessarily sin) that we are allowing to be part of our identity that should be eliminated.

As leaders I think this is one of the biggest coming-to-terms areas for us. What are we allowing to influence us that we shouldn't? These aren't always bad things, but sometimes certain good things are bad for us. As I said earlier, maybe we give too much authority to famous pastors or celebrities. We try to change how we preach, dress, or act to be more like them. It may be that we listen to too much secular music in order to be relevant to our young people and are not noticing how it is affecting our speech, outlook, or thoughts. It could be that we are giving too much time to watching sports and not enough time to praying. It could be overt sin, an ongoing struggle with pornography, or a secret craving for popularity or finances.

Taking time to honestly look at our lives and identify the things that are influencing us is important. God, and His Word, should have precedence over all other things. Any other thing we give authority to will eventually influence every part of us. We will begin to look like the things we give ourselves to.

Early on in my walk with the Lord, I was extremely into downhill mountain biking. This was something that carried over from before salvation that wasn't a bad thing. It was my identity and area of pride for me and gave me a great inroad with young people in our youth ministry. I had a nice bike, could hit all the big jumps, and was known for this area in my life. At that time, I was busy dealing with other huge areas in my life, and this seemed to be a good way to stay active. I remember when during a worship service the Lord spoke to me and asked me to sell my bike and give up mountain biking. It was an identity that was taking the place of the identity that God wanted to work in me. I was shocked. I argued with my conscience for a while and finally gave in to the fact that it was God. I walked over to a guy that was mentoring me at the time and through tears told Him that God wanted me to sell my bike. He laughed at first but when he realized that it was a serious thing for me, he prayed and encouraged me. I didn't even have my bike on the market for a few days before someone came and bought it. I had to give up one identity in order for God to give me a piece of His.

God not only wants to give us His identity, but He wants to remove the wrong things that are taking His place in our lives. As leaders that work with other people, we have to be careful that the desire to gain influence with them never takes the place of God Himself having influence in us. To love and care for people is one of our highest goals, but it is not more important than our relationship with the Lord and Him changing us into His image.

> For what will it profit a man if he gains the whole world, and loses his own soul? Or what will a man give in exchange for his soul? (Mark 8:36–37, NKJV)

3. We should identify some attainable goals that God wants us to begin to pursue in being more like Him and the person He wants us to be.

Choosing a few areas that we can practically start walking out is a way to put action to our faith. We should choose attainable things, and unless we are Christ incarnate, we shouldn't attempt them all at once.

I wanted to be better known as an approachable youth pastor and believed that God was calling me to do so. One thing that the voice of the Lord (through my wife) suggested I could do was to be more present during in-between times in our youth services. So for a season, instead of retreating to my office to work after our service ended, I sat at the receptionist desk in our lobby after every service. As young people left, some came and said good-bye, and others stood around and began to talk to me. After only a few weeks, several whom I had struggled to make connections with came and sat down with me to talk. I'm still doing this, and I think I am becoming more approachable. My identity is changing into more of what God would have for me.

It feels awkward sometimes to change and do things differently, especially with those around who know you the best. Changing our identity starts with just that—change! What are some things that you can begin to change today? Even if you try a hundred times and fail. What are those things that you can begin to walk out and see God work His way in you?

4. We must simply begin to walk it out!

When all is said and done, it ultimately comes down to simply starting somewhere and deciding to make a change. My prayer in writing this book was that leaders and nonleaders alike would feel stirred to solidify their identity and continue to discover who God designed each of them to be. Just like Peter, there came a moment when Jesus had gone to heaven and he was left with the choice to either walk in His newness or retreat back to where he once was before Christ encountered him. He had to simply decide that he was going to be the person God wanted him to be.

I have been told since I was young that what counts the most is what we do when no one is looking. When everyone else leaves and it is just us, those are the moments when we truly learn to walk in our new identity. Christ is always there to walk with us, but we do have to learn to be people of integrity when it comes to our identity. Integrity is often talked about in regards to finances or purity. We need to be people of integrity when growing our identity as well. Can we walk in newness when no one is looking? Are we only smiling and showing Christ when people are around, or does our new identity also follow us home?

As leaders, people who aren't as far down the road as we are surround us. One of our goals is to help them grow closer to God and for them to find their place in serving Him. I believe it is so important that we know who we are so that we can help others discover who they are. As God shows us different aspects of what He wants us to be, I pray that we will seek Him more, believe in faith, and step out of the boat to be those who walk in our God-given identity. We should never look back. As we grow in the things God sets in front of us, we should grab as many as we can along the way and help them walk this journey too. Who has God made you to be? Get a glimpse, and run as hard as you can after it.

> Therefore we also, since we are surrounded by so great a cloud of witnesses, let us lay aside every weight, and the sin which so easily ensnares us, and let us run with endurance the race that is set before us, looking unto Jesus, the author and finisher of our faith, who for the joy that was set before Him endured the cross, despising the shame,

and has sat down at the right hand of the throne of God.
(Heb. 12:1–2, NKJV)

Walking in godly identity is one of the best experiences of life. Learning why we were made the way we were and how that fits into the things God has called us to do is so incredibly fulfilling. We need to heed Paul's counsel in this verse and run, not merely walk, toward these things! We need to lay aside the things that keep us back and negatively influence all that we are and set our sights on what God has created us to be. We must acknowledge and understand that others are watching our lives as an example for their own lives. As we run, others will follow and begin to find their God-given identity as well.

I have tried to walk these things out in my own life. I had a burden to write this book because it has been one of my biggest areas of battle. Being a leader is not easy. I have struggled with the dual pressure of being a leader as well as growing in my own walk in the process. One of the hardest seasons on my journey was when I was trying to serve while also trying to be what I perceived others wanted me to be. I kept failing because I was trying to fulfill another person's identity spoken for me. Like Peter, I couldn't figure out why nothing was working. It was then that the Lord asked me, "Who am I asking you to be?" At first my answer was what other people had said but not what the Lord had said. I realized then that I hadn't heard directly from Him the answer to that question.

Once Peter really heard from God who he was meant to be, his life drastically changed. In the first few chapters of the book of Acts, we read about some of Peter's first steps as a brand-new man. Jesus ascended to heaven, and Peter, full of the Holy Spirit, preached. And three thousand people got saved in one meeting! Peter actually became a fisher of men—not in words alone but in powerful actions.

I'm still learning, and I pray that I never stop. I have an idea of who that person is whom God is asking me to be. Like Peter, I do not want to just know who God is calling me to be; I also want to take steps of obedience. One of the pieces is writing books. So you are literally reading my first step in this direction. I pray that once you close this book, there will be a fresh step that you can take. You are going to do great things! It starts with one question…

Who are you?

Made in the USA
San Bernardino, CA
07 June 2017